MILLIONAIRES' ISLANDS

Also by Willi Frischauer

TWILIGHT IN VIENNA

THE NAZIS AT WAR

GOERING

HIMMLER

THE NAVY'S HERE (with Robert Jackson)

THE MAN WHO CAME BACK

EUROPEAN COMMUTER

GRAND HOTELS OF EUROPE

ONASSIS

THE AGA KHANS

DAVID FROST

Willi Frischauer

MILLIONAIRES'
ISLANDS

London
MICHAEL JOSEPH

First published in Great Britain by Michael Joseph Ltd
52 Bedford Square, London, W.C.1
1973

7181 1070 6

Set and printed in Great Britain
by Tonbridge Printers Ltd, Tonbridge, Kent,
in Baskerville eleven on thirteen point,
on paper supplied by P. F. Bingham Ltd
and bound by James Burn at Esher, Surrey

CONTENTS

ILLUSTRATIONS

INTRODUCTION

So many of the outstanding Greek shipowners prefer to conduct their highly remunerative business in secrecy that, to acknowledge the help I have received in my Odyssey around the Aegean and Ionian islands, my excursions into the undergrowth of the City of London and the canyons of Manhattan, might embarrass people to whom I owe some valuable information. I have talked personally to all – well, almost all – my subjects, but the conversations, though invariably amicable, did not always produce the material I wanted, forcing me to pursue my inquiries along other than the familiar shipping lanes.

There is some ambiguity here, because, alongside the almost pathological determination of some to keep out of the public gaze, I encountered others who seek the bright rays of publicity – as long as it reflects favourably on them. Not a few suffered from a mild form of schizophrenia and wanted to have it both ways. To balance the contradictory influences was not always easy.

Thus, the names and background of some who were anxious to be included in this (very personal) selection have been omitted. Others who put the greatest obstacles in my way will find that their reticence has only whetted my appetite. But even they will, I hope, admit that I have tried to do them justice. On the whole, I have come away at the end of my work with a great regard for most, and affection for some, of the shipping men who figure in these pages.

Personal selection! This is an idiosyncratic account which tries to embrace the historical background as well as the professional, financial, personal and social activities of the Greek shipowners. I have concentrated on those who seem to me characteristic and whose history and current affairs lend themselves to the kind of treatment I had in mind. My choice of islands and personalities, therefore, does not imply any judg-

ment on their importance or ranking in Greek and world
shipping which is almost synonymous.

Neither does this book claim to be a complete history of
Greek shipping – Andrea Lemos, that splendid and venerable
shipowner, naval historian and member of an old island family,
has produced a mountain of learned volumes on the subject
which I have been permitted to mine for nuggets of information.

Apart from his work, I have consulted many other sources,
particularly family histories which Greek shipping clans
produce with diligence and gusto, none more attractive and
illuminating than Elias Kulukundis' *Journey to a Greek Island*
(Cassell, London, 1968). I have interviewed scores of people
associated with events, past and recent, on which I touch. The
help of my friends Giorgios Alciades and Anthony Zimbalis
in Athens has been invaluable since they took up many matters
which I failed to trace on my numerous visits to Greece. In
New York, London and Lausanne others have enabled me
to fill the gaps. Greek shipping journals like *Naftika Chronika*,
Krikos, *Hellenic Shipping* and *Surveyor*, the publication of the
American Bureau of Shipping, have stimulated ideas and
opened many vistas.

None of them, nobody in fact who talked to me, can claim
any credit or need accept any blame for the use I have made
of their information. This is entirely my own responsibility.
Friends and enemies of Greece alike will find much to carp
about. Controversy is a strong element in the Greek mental
makeup, and in this respect, as in other national characteristics,
Greek shipowners, at home or abroad, conform to the pattern.

Looking back on a year's hard slog, I confess that it was
pleasant work. The meetings with the islanders on their home
ground or in their western abodes was most enjoyable. It was
a round of yachting trips, launchings and other parties,
stimulating talk – a lot of talk.

My aim was to reflect it with its peculiar flavour of history,
endeavour, pride, nostalgia, business and social gossip. No
more, no less.

Willi Frischauer

London, 1972

I
HOME ARE THE SAILORS

WAR, women and wealth, said Lord Northcliffe, make the most riveting news. By this token there is nothing to beat the Greek shipowners. They command the front pages, and the mystery in which their operations and their movements are often shrouded generates gossip in a dozen languages – among themselves they are the brightest gossips in creation. The sea, trade, history – and not only the turbulent history of Greece – weave the colourful backcloth against which they perform. Their stories and their yachts take us on voyages of adventure to the tiny islands from which they spring and to which their children and children's children remain loyal.

They take us back to the Turkish empire of the Ottomans from which their forefathers, turning sailing boats into fighting ships, liberated Greece in the War of Independence of 1821. They forged a link with the old Russia of the czars with whom they traded. Today there are few countries with a coastline which their ships do not visit. Citizens of the world, they remain Greek to the core, whatever the colour of their passports. The United States, Britain, France, Switzerland have embraced many of them and have profited handsomely from their financial acumen.

Rich as Croesus, cunning, fleet-footed (and fertile) as Hermes, these restless wanderers – by jet not by ship – have carried the aura of Odysseus into our times. In the space of three or four generations they have sailed triumphantly from rags to riches, taming rough and hostile seas in combined efforts of whole families brought together by sight-unseen brides and their generous dowries. When the need arises they stand together as one man. They treat their quarrels as discreet family affairs and look down on Onassis and Niarchos who allow the public to gloat over their disputes. Others are loth to weaken the chain of common heritage which, whatever else divides them, anchors Chios and Ithaca, Siros, Andros and Cephalonia in the same three-thousand years old seafaring tradition.

Embattled masters of the waves and the counting house, they save their ships in violent storms or collect insurance when they lose them in war and peace. In the two great conflagrations of this century they carried the cargoes of war across the Atlantic and the Pacific. The second world war all but wiped out the Greek merchant navy built up by the sweat, skill, endurance and sacrifice of the captains who earned their stripes sailing before the mast. By 1945, the Greek fleet counted no more than one hundred and fifty ships or less than 600,000 tons. The United States came to the rescue by making a hundred ships available which became the nucleus of the Greek-owned merchant fleet, fourth biggest in the world and growing – albeit under many flags – to an estimated thirty-seven million tons by 1972. The Greek Government will not rest until every Greek owned ship flies the Greek flag.

This spectacular expansion has brought legendary wealth to the leading Greek shipping families, some hundred-and-forty of them, who between them own most of the Greek tonnage afloat. The seafaring captains from claustrophobically small islets like Oinoussai (pop. 1,580) have fathered captains of industry whose fortunes are counted in hundreds of millions of dollars. The sea tang which attached to previous generation, – the original Lemos, Livanos, Kulukundis, (Hadji) Paterass Goulandris – is diffused by the wafts of Dior, Guerlain, Marcel Rochas who anoint and robe the ladies of the species. Only a few of the epigones are lost to the ancient craft and have ventured into the arts (theatre, literature, history) which some of their elders used to bemoan as a sad waste of traditional talent. But most of them collect art treasures, race horses, real estate as avidly as ships.

When they meet together – and, however great the rivalry,

they always meet – the talk is of ships, ships, ships, marriage (and the occasional divorce), of big coups and bigger money, of money and Greek politics which means money when they are on the winning side – more often than not the biggest among them hedge their bets and back every horse in the race. The gossip rarely ventures far beyond the fraternity. There is no need to. So much happens all the time. To all of them.

Gregarious and hospitable, they love parties, seal some of their spectacular deals with a handshake at *El Morocco* or *Annabel's*. They launch their giant tankers to the clinking of glasses, toast the success of their professional associations which they launch as prolifically, celebrate shipping exhibitions and charity drives with the same inveterate enthusiasm and entertain public men at private parties which are culinary and conversational feasts.

For a swift wholesale introduction to the most legendary of them, dollar for dollar, ton for ton, personality for personality, there could have been no better occasion than *Posidonia, 70*, the international shipping exhibition in Athens, and no better place than the Royal Yacht Club overlooking Tourcolimano Harbour with its hundreds of yachts swaying in the gentle breeze – though, when young King Constantine left the country in 1967, the name of his favourite Sunday lunch hide-out was changed to National Yacht Club.

Professor Ioannis Holevas, the Junta's Minister of Shipping at the time, played host to a distinguished gathering. His guests were the Greek shipowners who converged on Athens from their New York penthouses, their London mansions and their Swiss lakeside retreats – from *xenitia* (exile) where most of them made their fortunes. Whatever you may think of the Greek Colonels, their ships have certainly come home.

It did not even matter that Onassis and Niarchos were not there. Big as they are, they remain outsiders, 'parachutists' (in the parlance of the traditional Greeks) who have dropped into the shipping business from the sky and do not really belong. Onassis, never one for public occasions, stayed put on his private island of Skorpios, a little peeved, so the gossips said, because a last-minute veto by President Nixon spoiled his plan to entertain a few American astronauts on *Christina*. Niarchos was missing because the authorities were still investigating his wife's tragic death on Spetsopoula Island. Seventeen year old Philip Niarchos manfully represented his father at official functions.

But Costa M. Lemos was there, the anonymous scion of a shipping family from the eastern outposts of Greece, hiding in a corner, sheltered by his coterie, trying as always to look unobtrusive and remain unrecognised as if those who mattered did not know him anyway. Lemos prefers power to publicity.

Ackimos Gratsos was there, representing Ithaca where the spirit of Odysseus is still alive – without his brother Costa, Onassis might never have mastered the shipping business. Manuel and John Kulukundis were there – John is the head of the London Greeks; and Manuel, tall, slim, aristocratic, as becomes the doyen of the shipping industry from the islands of Kasos and Siros, had made the trip from New York. Youthfully alert, he did not betray his seventy years, most of them devoted to Greek shipping which he helped to resurrect after the second world war. Minos and Joseph Colocotronis were there, descendants of the nineteenth century freedom fighter from the Peloponnese, living proof, if proof were needed, that it was still possible to amass a multi-million dollar fleet within the last decade.

The Island of Andros has brought forth shipping clans galore but none more impressive and prominent the world over than the proliferating Goulandrises whose fortunes rival that of Onassis and who were represented by Alexander Goulandris, a member of the younger generation. John A. Hadjipateras having departed for Italy on shipping business, his brother Costa showed the flag of the fabulous Pateras-Hadjipateras family which has done so much to make the miniscule islet of Oinoussai a gold-lined cradle of Greek shipping.

Japanese heads popped up on all sides. The Greeks are the best customers of their shipyards and 250,000 ton tankers roll off their production lines like motorcars from a Detroit conveyor belt. German ship builders from Hamburg, Bremen and Kiel touted for business, and the English from the Clyde, the Tyne and Belfast were there on a similar errand – there was much talk about the PS14's produced by Austin & Pickersgill, the Sunderland shipyards which happen to belong to an 'English' Greek.

A day or so later at the Athens *Hilton* I was once more engulfed in a sea of nautical magnates when Minos and Joseph Colocotronis threw a party for which the Aegean seemed to have given up most of its lobsters and the Champagne some of its finest vintages. The multi-lingual conversation was deceptively casual and the social mating of builders and owners was bound to produce thousands of tons of shipping. Now and then the hosts looked over their shoulders towards the doors so as not to miss the arrival of Colonel-in-Chief Premier George Papadopoulos who had promised an appearance but did not make it – members of the Greek Junta rarely turn up when they are announced and are rarely announced when they turn up. Next morning only a handful of us were present when the bustling, baldheaded Colonel Patakos, the Junta's Number Two, visited the Greek shipping exhibition at the crack of dawn long before the public was admitted.

The scene shifts to yet another party, this time at a magnificent apartment high up on Lycabitou facing the majestic Acropolis at window level. The hosts – Andrea G. Lemos, rich and erudite veteran of shipping, politics and literature, twice a member of parliament, qualified lawyer, sea captain before he was thirty, a maritime historian of considerable stature, and his wife Maria, like most wives of Greek shipowners, a shipowner's daughter – a Carras from the island of Chios.

To a Greek, a ship is like a woman (to the British it spells adventure, to the Norwegian sound business) and he lavishes all his affections on 'her' – I am not sure but I suspect that the Greeks coined the expression 'a ship's husband' for the man who looks after her in port. Perhaps this is why Maria

Lemos and the ladies seemed reconciled to the conversation which, wherever it strayed, invariably reverted to their rivals for their husbands' affection – ships.

Like the ships which sail the oceans the table talk sailed in rhythmic flow from Greece to Britain and the United States. Each of these owners had a son, a brother, a cousin running his office in London and New York. Their daughters, speaking English or French as accent-free and fluently as Greek, brought with them the flavour of Mrs Hewitt's Classes, of English colleges and Swiss finishing schools. Politely, patiently, indulgently they listened – one suspects for the hundredth time – to anecdotes which are the stock in trade of their elders who fondly caress the names of their native islands and speak with possessive pride of the hardy, austere, thrifty old seadogs who laid the foundations of their fortunes.

The tables were groaning under plates of octopus and prawns and every culinary delicacy as they nostalgically recalled the gruff sailor who bawled out his son for wasting his pennies on a pat of butter when he ought to have contributed them to the family hoard towards another, bigger vessel. They giggled handsomely about the story, retold for my benefit, about another captain who took a single egg aboard, promised it secretly to every deckhand in turn if he really put his back into the work, and extracted the maximum effort from his men by whispering into their ears: 'You, with the egg . . . if you want it you will have to try a little harder!'

This was the spirit in which the old ones went to sea on the meagrest of rations, each member of the family lending a hand without pay, sons, brothers, neighbours and fellow islanders investing their hard labour and their savings, and if their efforts did not add up to the price of a new ship, two or three captains pooling their resources which is how some of the most flourishing partnerships originated. In those days safety was often at a premium beyond a captain's reach, relaxation a rare luxury when ships returned to home ports after months on distant high seas, and a honeymoon ended the day after a hopeful groom had carried his bride across the porch. The Meissen plates off which we supped, the heavy silver cutlery, the crystal classes and the old masters on the walls, the half dozen waiters who served the food and poured the wine at the Lemos party were a far cry from those days. Yet, the tradition lingered and lured and had to be pursued to its source.

Next morning my host and his friends were back at the headquarters of their empires at Pireaus and, while tourists flocked to the ruins of ancient Greek temples, I went sight-seeing among the cathedrals of the contemporary Greek gods who answer to the names of Lemos, Livanos, Goulandris or Onassis and Niarchos, the more recently created deities. Akti Miaouli which sounds like the plaintive cry of a kitten is the heart of Greek shipping. Along King Constantine Quay between St Spiridon and St Nicola Church some of the most imposing office blocks have sprung up in the last ten years.

Among them are the Livanos Building (the late Stavros Niarchos was at one time father-in-law of both Onassis and Niarchos), the Nomikos and Goulandris powerhouses and, just round the corner, the 'Springfield' block which sur-prisingly, turns out to be the Onassis head office. Niarchos' headquarters are at Skaramanga Bay, but big branches of the Chase Manhattan, the First National and the Bank of Nova Scotia dwell cheek by jowl with the shipowners to whom they owe much of their business. The Lemos Maritime Building rises high over the inner harbour.

By contrast the building at Passalimani which I visited is drab and inconspicuous except for the blue-jacketed, armed sailors of the Greek Coastguards at the narrow entrance. Known as 'Three M's' – Ministry of Merchant Marine – it is the hub of the frantic and spectacular Greek shipping policy. The minis-terial offices on the second floor are austere – accustomed to more lavish surroundings, visiting shipowners must feel hemmed in in these cramped quarters. Aides-de-camp wear naval uniform, speak fluent English and run the outer office with strict military discipline. Successive Ministers of Marine

17

have been the Pied Pipers who have lured Greek shipowners and their ships back from their profitable *xenitia* under Central American flag of convenience.

It is an astonishing accomplishment and enables Greece, so desperately poor for decades while Greek shipowners prospered in the tax free havens of Panama, Honduras and Liveria, to offer them the flag of convenience of their own country.

Flag of Convenience – Flag of Expediency or Flag of Necessity – used to be a term of contempt among American and British shipowners suggesting low standards of safety, low pay and poor conditions for sailors, an old-fashioned idea as Onassis explained to me with conviction. No modern shipowner in his senses, he said, would entrust a tanker worth ten million dollars or more to inferior or indented sailors. No major insurance company – invariably English or American – would underwrite a ship operating under any but the most up-to-date conditions. Competition for competent Greek seamen is such that, like soldiers of a modern army, they would not serve on ships unless assured of safety, comfort and decent wages.

Just think of it – a ship worth ten million dollars with a crew of thirty means that, as units of economic value, each member of the crew is responsible for a staggering 333,000 dollars. What other working man handles a third of a million dollars worth of equipment? And, as Costa Lemos says, a ship is only as good as the men who sail it.

It so happens that the Greek Junta came to power in 1967 at the time when the Arab-Israeli war closed the Suez Canal once more. Ships were forced to take the long route round the Cape which caused a tremendous demand for tankers and every other sort of vessel. Freight rates shot up offering a rich harvest to Greek shipowners who went to work with a vengeance. They commissioned a staggering eleven and a half million tons of new ships, the following year ordered another two hundred and ten vessels, many of them tankers in the 150,000 to 220,000 ton class.

'Let's get these Greek-owned ships under the Greek flag!' the new Greek Government decided. Taxes on Greek-flag

vessels were reduced to the level of the traditional flags of convenience countries – what they save in tax the Greeks invest
in still more ships. Favourable credit facilities for vessels built
in Greek shipyards brought orders and employment. A start
was made with improving communications and a programme
of expansion of training centres for officers and seamen
initiated (although Greece still has a long way to go before
catching up with the demand). 1969 was proclaimed 'The
Year of Greek Shipping'. Three million tons of Greek shipping
returned to Greece making a total of over eleven million tons
flying the blue and white ensign with the white cross. By early
1972 the total tonnage under the Greek flag had risen to
15,800,000 and was growing at the rate of nearly 100,000 a
month.

Over one hundred and twenty firms established headquarters in Greece. Onassis transferred several ships to the
Greek flag. Niarchos expanded his Skaramanga shipyard;
Professor Stratis G. Andreadis, the tough shipping-shipbuild-
ing-insurance-banking tycoon from Chios, created Eleusis
Shipyard, near Athens and is still expanding it. A new Goulandris shipyard came into being with Krupp's of Germany
providing some of their know-how and their steel. Everything
is humming. In New York, the American Bureau of Shipping
is straining every muscle to strengthen its business with the
Greeks – the Bureau's Greek Technical Committee includes
every Greek shipowner worth his salt. Blow for blow, Lloyds
of London are following suit.

Even the run-down of the American involvement in Vietnam which would release American shipping for international
trade, would make much difference for some time ahead. Oil
consumption was growing and the oil being carried from
source to consumer. World trade was relying on ships to keep
the cargoes moving. As nations come together across thousands
of miles of ocean, as ships grew towards and beyond the
million ton mark, the outlook for shipping, apart from
occasional brief setbacks, was as good as ever.

*   *   *

Sipping my steaming sweet Turkish coffee in the spacious lounge of the *Hotel Grande Bretagne* in the heart of Athens, the turbulent British Army headquarters during the civil war of 1944, I heard a page boy's thin voice piping reverently but insistently: 'Mr Lemos please – Mr Lemos to the telephone!' Five men at five different tables rose, made themselves known and started towards the telephone booth. They were all Lemos, all shipowners and – *ca va sans dire* – millionaires (and Costa M. Lemos was not even present). There was Leon Lemos, all 280 pounds of him; Andrea Lemos, Polydorvs Lemos, Mayor of Oinoussai; Adamantios Lemos and Panaghos Lemos who belong to different branches and were on a visit from London.

Clinging to Panaghos Lemos was his little boy, English prep school written all over him, chatting away in the accents of Mayfair: 'I brought him here to learn Greek,' his father said. That's *xenitia* for you! Born and reared in England, the boy comes to Greece every year to practise the language of his ancestors and absorb the atmosphere and tradition of their country. Whether they settle and prosper in England or the United States, descendants of the early Greek seafarers want their children to remain Greek. Except for the Irish and the Jews, no other ex-patriates remain so firmly wedded to their country of origin and, above all, to their islands.

II

RICHER THAN ONASSIS

A DRAB day in March 1969. Twenty prosperous gentlemen, some accompanied by aides, file into the big hall of the Greek Orthodox Church in the City of London – like Islam the Greek Church is closely involved in the lives and livelihood of the faithful. The twenty are Greeks, most of them from the tiny island of Oinoussai, a few from neighbouring Chios. All of them are shipowners controlling between them two hundred and twenty ships, altogether some four million tons worth well over £100 million.

They are there in response to a letter which sets out the revolutionary changes in the shipping industry during the last few years when companies merged and pooled resources creating the new mammoth shipping groups. Togetherness is the theme of the letter – they, too, would have to come together, as it were, under the flag of Oinoussai. Lemos Pateras, Hadjipateras interests are represented. Other big names present are Colocotronis, Xylas and Carras.

'A hundred years ago', the letter points out, 'our forefathers, inhabitants of our beloved island, when faced with the problems of insuring their sailing ships in the international market, decided to form their own insurance company. Though, by modern standards, they could be described as 'uneducated', they proved that they had a deeper understanding of their situation and of the need for co-operation than we who are businessmen of the twentieth century. To that they owed their survival'.

The twenty men responded promptly. There and then, in the Greek church hall in the City of London, they decide to form a new organisation. A new pool, known as Oinoussian

21

Maritime Limited, comes into being and is registered in London. Another huge shipping group is born.

One son of Oinoussai kept aloof because his own shipping group was already so big that there was not much point merging it with others. Costa M. Lemos is richer than Onassis, owns a fleets of six million tons and controls assets of 750 million dollars or therabouts. Like most Greek tycoons, this Sidney Greenstreet of the shipping trade, big-faced, heavy, slow-moving, likes to surround himself with mystery and nurses his trade secrets like a jealous father nurses a child prodigy. Lemos operates in an atmosphere reminiscent of Greta Garbo or Howard Hughes. The result is a Lemos legend of sorts, although legends have a dream-like quality which Costa M. Lemos totally lacks. But he is a typical Oinoussian linked to his native island by a modern Greek tragedy.

The stage for it was set with the Nazi invasion of Greece in 1941 which caught his ageing father, Michael C. Lemos, on the mainland separated from his two sons and his daughter who were living in England and America. Greek family bonds transcend war and conquest. Costa Lemos was not prepared to leave his father under the German yoke. In the best Greek tradition, he decided to mount a naval rescue operation to extract the old gentleman from the Nazi occupied country. The plan was to take him to Egypt, first stage in the escape route of many Greeks in the years of occupation, and on to London.

It was arranged for Lemos senior to make his way to his native Oinoussai to wait for help to arrive. The island, as we shall see, suffered all the horrors Germans inflicted on subjugated countries and old Michael Lemos suffered with his fellow islanders. Before his son's helping hand could reach out for him, his span of life ran out. Denied a peaceful retirement in the western world, he must yet have died content in the knowledge that he would rest in peace on Oinoussai.

Greek shipowners live on through their ships and the ships of their heirs, and Costa M. Lemos would never be without a ship that does not honour his father's name. It is not only on the headstone of his grave in Oinoussai that the name of Michael C. Lemos is writ large. In October 1970 it appeared again in outsize lettering decorating the bows of his son's latest 200,000 ton super tanker which was launched at the A. G. Weser shipyards in Bremen, North Germany. The *Michael C. Lemos* was the biggest ship ever to sail under the Greek flag.

She joined the huge fleet of tankers, bulk carriers and tramps of the C. M. Lemos Group which is growing fast as new super tankers – twelve of them on order or twice as many as Onassis commissioned over the same period – come off the launching pads of German and Japanese shipyards. They account for the awe in which Lemos is held by the trade while the public at large is hardly aware of his existence.

As if Greek shipowners do not arrange their meetings with journalists to some good, though not immediately apparent purpose, Costa M. Lemos managed to look surprised when Stephen Aris, the enterprising and well-known financial writer, tracked him down in London. 'How did you know I was here? I thought nobody knew me', Lemos said disingenuously as he admitted the visitor to his permanent penthouse suite at *Claridge's Hotel* where the equally elusive Stavros Niarchos is his neighbour.

A personal encounter does not throw much light on the portrait of this smoothly and silently ticking human business machine which, like any stripped down computer, still leaves the uninitiated none the wiser. Costa M. Lemos is a non-personality reminiscent of the perfectly-camouflaged war-time surface raiders whose engine power and hidden guns were a match for any destroyer.

With an intellectual snobbism, not uncommon among financial and industrial magnates, he only opens up among people he accepts as his equals – presidents of major American insurance companies, chairmen of big banks, shipyard owners, Greek cabinet ministers or members of the U.S. administration. With fellow shipowners he maintains friendly contact –

at least superficially. When he meets Onassis, they talk and talk without giving anything away.

His conversation, not exactly inspired, is searching rather than stimulating. What Lemos collects as avidly as ships, property and cash is – information. He likes to hear the grass grow, find out about industrial developments before they happen, about new financing techniques before they are perfected, about technical advances before they are prepared and about political situations before they arise. A man without small talk or interest in the idle gossip which delights other ship-owners, he has reached the age of sixty without ever having been heard discussing women.

So much to do, too little time. Where other owners leave technicalities to their executives, Lemos studies them himself with the expertise of a trained engineer; where others consult two dozen lawyers, Lemos prefers to dissect complicated legal problems on his own; where Onassis, for instance, lives and works by intuition Lemos is the cool and calculating expert at all times: 'No other man in our industry has the knowledge which is Costa Lemos' greatest asset,' says Costa Gratsos who is no mean shipping expert himself. Other shipowners can be scathing about his single-minded dedication to business, few deny him their admiration, albeit often tinged with envy. But even those who are envious of his success admit that he has earned his good and great fortune.

So what does he do with it? Like a Prussian he regards work as its own reward and continues to work even at social functions and through meals in intimate restaurants (like John Stais' famous *White Tower* in London's Bloomsbury). He has no hobbies? He is hard put to name any. He loves the sea where he spends what little leisure he allows himself: 'I like to sail and can forget all my problems when I am at sea,' he says, '. . . it is as restful as returning home.' Has he, then, a yacht like the *Christina* on which Onassis relaxes, or a famous schooner ike the *Creole* which is Niarchos' pride and joy? 'Costa Lemos would not have a ship that does not earn money,' a fellow shipowner says with conviction.

Not for him the leisurely cruises in the Caribbean or even the Aegean and Ionian seas which the seafaring Greeks criss-cross forever when they have time on their hands. Not for him the racing yawls in which the younger generation test their skill and their stamina; 'You put all your genius in your life," Costa Gratsos once told him.

The trouble with this able super-sailor is that he has never learned to play. Like many old Greek sea captains his father, Michael C. Lemos, was demanding and wanted his son to have the kind of education he himself never enjoyed. The art of leisure was not greatly appreciated in Oinoussai in the early decades of the century and the hard school in which the young Costa M. Lemos was brought up became a way of life.

It was not enough for him and his brother Adamantios to become sailors which, for a Lemos, was like learning to walk. From the moment Costa was despatched to school in Athens it was work, work, work for the little fellow. After leaving gymnasium (high school) he was enrolled at Athens University Law School and studied engineering at the same time. Even so, his real test was yet to come.

A twenty-five million dollar block on Third Avenue which he owns is the New York headquarters of his 'Triton Shipping Company'. Sitting at his highly polished desk, he often looks over his shoulder at the model of *S.S. Adamas* – a half model really, the mirror behind completing the picture – which he values more than the models of his biggest vessels: 'It's the ship on which I started my training,' he says with a tinge of nostalgia which takes him back to the late twenties. By modern standards, *S.S. Adamas*, built in England in 1918, looks small and insignificant: 'I served in her for six years.' Costa Lemos recalls. They were hard years during which he worked in every department of the ship claiming no privileges. The reward at the end of this rigorous training was the Master's Certificate which he added to his law and engineering degrees.

With brother Adam, he joined his father's firm which operated a respectable fleet out of England but did not belong to the big league. While their father went to live in Athens, the brothers (like other Greek shipowners) and their sister Maria moved to the United States soon after the outbreak of war when it became difficult to conduct operations from the British Isles under siege by Luftwaffe, U-boats and enemy surface raiders. The *S.S. Adamas* was soon lost and her fate was shared by every ship the Lemos family called their own. Ten million dollars worth of their tonnage went to the bottom of the sea.

The débâcle of the Greek merchant fleet in the allied war service hit Lemos even harder than other Greeks. He emerged from the war as a shipowner without a single ship. Though the blow was softened by compensation from the insurance companies, Costa Lemos had to start from scratch.

The shortage of shipping at the end of the war was acute. Tonnage was tied up carrying American aid to war-ravaged Eurpe. Continental shipyards were in ruins and the few on either side of the Atlantic which had escaped damage were booked up with orders for years ahead. Ships were hard to come by. When the United States made a hundred Liberty ships available to the Greeks, Costa obtained one of them and named it *Michail* – after his father. He put down 135,000 dollars which was twenty-five per cent of the purchasing price, the rest to be paid over eighteen years under guarantee by the Greek Government. The second rise of the Lemos fortunes was at hand.

For the Greeks, the American Liberty ships were a licence to print money and Costa Lemos was not long content with only one of them. Onassis pioneered a finance formula – promptly followed by Niarchos and adopted by other Greeks – which helped to overcome the traditional reluctance of American banks to loan money on ships, particularly on Greek ships. The idea – 'like the egg of Columbus" – seemed simple and obvious. Having raised the down payment of twenty-five per cent of the ship's cost, the secret was to find an oil company to charter the vessel for two, three or more voyages and to use the charter party (contract) as security for the remaining seventy-five per cent. A few trips later – such is the finance of shipping – the vessels had earned the bulk of the outstanding amount.

The procedure was repeated with the next ship, the third and the fourth, and soon with whole series of new construction. Once the finance institutes realised how skilfully and profitably Greeks operated their ships, the floodgates of credit were opened and billions of dollars poured forth. Heavily mortgaged for short periods, the ships did not only recoup their cost but made tremendous fortunes for their owners and the banks and insurance companies which put up the money. This is how Costa Lemos and the other Greek shipowners laid the foundations of their post-war fleets and made them grow.

Parting company from his brother, businesswise – Adam Lemos was none too happy about the separation and the manner in which it came about – Costa M. Lemos sailed on alone, but not for long. Sister Maria married *Megaleas* (Big) Goulandris – John P. Goulandris, eldest of the second generation of the shipping family from Andros (whom we shall get to know better before long), and Costa Lemos joined forces with his brother-in-law in new shipping ventures which prospered. On his own account and in partnership with *Megaleas*, Lemos acquired more Liberty ships and soon graduated to 16,500 ton T2 tankers. He created the Triton Shipping Company, the hub of his activities, and never looked back.

If there is a good wife behind every successful executive, there is a good aide behind every flourishing shipowner. Costa M. Lemos owes much of his rapid progress to two fellow Oinoussians, both hardy sea captains who joined him in the United States after the war. The Mavrophillipas brothers – Captain A (for Argherinos) and Captain John as they are known in the trade – worked tirelessly for the boss and grew rich in the process. Captain A returned to Greece to start his own fleet, Captain John remained with Costa Lemos in New York.

Though swift, progress was not smooth. Freight rates and business fluctuated wildly and it required courage and judgment to stay on top – judgment to buy when the price of ships was low and courage to hold on until good times returned. Luck played a part. The trick was to have ships available for charter when rates were high yet not to be left with too many when the bottom dropped out of the market: 'Shipping is like the sea itself,' Costa M. Lemos says. 'If you have calm weather now, you can be sure that rough weather is ahead.' Shipping is not a speculative business he hastens to add – if it was thought to be, those who finance vast building programmes might be afraid to get their feet wet. Lemos has an answer: 'When it is good sailing you have to prepare for bad times.'

In 1948, he took time off from the hectic round of conferences, ship inspections and transatlantic trips which made the pattern of his life. He was in his mid-thirties, time to get married and have an heir. The girl of his choice was pretty Evi Dambassis, needless to say the daughter of a Greek shipowner – from the island of Andros. They were married in New York but Costa was not the man to let a little thing like marriage distract him from business. The honeymoon was spent in Los Angeles but it was not the glamour of Hollywood that attracted the bridegroom. Costa M. Lemos had business with the local shipyards, which kept him busy most of the time. No wonder the romance was short-lived. There was no heir, Evi departed and the marriage was dissolved, before it had rightly started.

Three years later, Costa fell in love with Melpo Pateras, daughter of a shipping family from his own island of Oinoussai, who was twenty years younger than he and certain to give him a son and heir before long.

Their first child was a girl, named Chryssanti after Costa's mother, the next was a boy. Costa Lemos was jubilant: 'Now I have a partner!' he greeted the new arrival. As is Greek custom, the boy was called Michael after his grandfather. (Soon there was another girl, Irene.) Baby Michael became the partner in a prosperous business. In spite of periodical ups and downs Costa and his son were literally riding on the crest of the ocean waves. Their empire grew more substantial every year.

When the Korean war forced the United States to employ

the bulk of their merchant shipping to transport war materials to the distant battlefields, foreigners were left to fill the gaps in the shipping lanes of international trade. The boom swept Costa Lemos along to ever more profitable business. He needed more ships but American yards were chock-a-block and Britain's prices and delivery dates were difficult. Undeterred he looked elsewhere for additional tonnage, and was one of the first to explore the facilities of Japanese shipyards. Not long ago he recalled how the Japanese quoted him a price £1 million lower than Swan and Hunter, the British shipbuilders. Besides Japanese delivery dates were up to two years shorter. In 1953 Costa Lemos placed his first order in Japan.

There was a recession in shipping at the end of the Korean War but when the British intervention in Egypt closed the Suez Canal in 1956, the demand for tankers and bulk carriers rose to new heights. One way or another Costa Lemos had his ships built until his fleet grew to a staggering six million tons, many of the ships carrying less mortgage than those of other owners.

His income from these 'complex moving masses', as he describes his modern super tankers, spread over dozens of companies and as many countries, is believed to be in excess of twenty million dollars a year, augmented by revenue from extensive real estate holdings and other enterprises outside shipping. His interests keep him on the move, gipsy-like, from country to country. With most of the American Greeks he shifted many of them from the United States when the Kennedy legislation on shipping and taxation complicated life for foreign owners.

When in New York, he stays with sister Kathy Zoullas, wife of a Greek industrialist, whom he installed in his own spacious Fifth Avenue apartment. Maria Goulandris, his other sister, occupies an apartment close by. Like all wealthy Greeks he maintains a house in Athens but his favourite house is his villa in Lausanne, Switzerland.

In London where he spends much of his time, giving a very good imitation of the 'invisible man', a custom-built Rolls-

Royce whisks him discreetly from *Claridge's* to the City. The car is not a status symbol – no need of that – but has taught him an important lesson which he passes on to all and sundry: 'A modern ship,' he says, "is like a Rolls-Royce. A bad driver or a bad maintenance man can ruin the finest Rolls-Royce in a few minutes. It is the same with ships – only much more expensive."

Firm and paternalistic in his approach, he runs his fleet like an emperor. A captain and engineer first, he draws the logical conclusions and regards his sailors as he regards his ships. Only the best are good enough for him. 'Our ships are only as good as the men who sail them,' he says. Unlike the old Greek captains who overworked and underpaid their crews, his sailors work under conditions and receive wages which keep their enthusiasm alive. He was one of the first Greeks to revert to the Greek flag and, though trade unions have taken a knock under the Junta, sailors serving on Lemos ships are not complaining.

Costa M. Lemos remains elusive and even close associates have difficulty in tracking him down. Yet, wherever he is, come Sunday morning, he goes to church. In London he worships at the Aghia Sophia, the Greek Orthodox Cathedral in Moscow Road, A genuinely devout man, he does not deserve the unkind remarks of fellow worshippers who have been heard to say: "What Costa Lemos prays for is – more ships!'

III

FROM SHEEP TO SHIPS

FIVE luminous rocks, barren except for grazing land, tiny specks in the sea within sight of the Turkish coast, home to fifteen hundred islanders – that's Oinoussai. The Greeks call it the Island of the Rich. These are the few square miles which have produced men like Costa M. Lemos; this is where the Pateras, Hadjipateras, Lyras and Mavrophillipas started on their 'beautiful journey' to fame and wealth.

Few Americans have ever heard of Oinoussai, few even of neighbouring Chios which is much bigger and claims to be Homer's birthplace. But long before Costa M. Lemos acquired his 250,000 ton tankers, his New York skyscraper and his reputation on Wall Street, these islands made an impact on the United States because what they grow – and grow in profusion – is *masticha* which keeps the jaws of Americans busy every day of their lives. Masticha is the stuff chewing gum is made of.

The Island of the Rich – one can hardly credit it, not at first glance – is picturesque and glows in the bright colours of the eastern Mediterranean. To reach it, I flew from Athens to Chios – the twenty-seater aircraft was a poor relation of the transatlantic jets of Onassis' Olympic Airways. From Chios a rickety old steamer chugs and stutters across the final stretch of water to the biggest of the five rocks which is Oinoussai. Scores of Greek shipowners, though most of them in their own yachts or motor launches, make the same trip every summer, returning to the island of their ancestors.

Where the old Oinoussians put up their little houses, square and squat, with tiled roofs and baking ovens in the courtyards, where they stalked in their Turkish pantaloons and skull caps – the women with hair in plaits, skirts down to their ankles, long-sleeved garments done up at the neck – the modern Greeks

31

have built their villas with elegant porticos, balconies and wall-to-wall windows. In summer this remote, idyllic Shangri-La, far from the beaten track of international tourists, is noisy with the English and American accents of their children and the Island of the Rich becomes an exclusive private club which only admits the sons and grandsons of Oinoussians.

They pay their subs with enthusiastic generosity, build churches, as if to expiate the sin of making so much money, and schools because their illiterate grandparents coveted an education as much as ships and worked their fingers to the bone to give their children what they themselves lacked.

A Pateras built the Naval Grammar School, and the Merchant Marine Officers Institute is the gift of London's Oinoussian shipowners – captains and cabin boys from Oinoussai contributed dollars and dimes. The monument of the Unrevealed Greek Sailor, a contribution from the Lemos family, bears the inscription, paraphrasing Pericles: 'To brave Sailors All Seas Are Home'.

The headstones in the graveyard read like a shipping register. Humble sailors and shipowners alike return to be buried in the hard soil of Oinoussai. The widow of Pandelis Lemos who died in 1957, financed a big block and gave it to the community. It houses the post office, the bank and the Nautical Museum which mirrors Oinoussai's history. How did it all start?

'It started with sheeps,' said Stefanos Lyras, the cheerful old ship's engineer with the sun-drenched weather-beaten face and a name that commands respect in shipping. Having sailed every ocean, he lives in retirement on his native island.

'You mean – ships?'

'No, sheeps,' he repeated in his Greek-accented English and pointed to a flock of sheep grazing on the hillside.

From sheep to ships!

The first to settle on Oinoussai came from the Chios village Kardamila looking for grazing land for their sheep which was about all there was on Oinoussai. They built their own boats to take wool and cheese back to Chios, to other islands and to Asia Minor. How their little caiques grew into millions of tons

of tankers and bulk carriers which plough the seas and harvest
fortunes for the sons of the island is a story which Oinoussians
never tire of exploring.

Greeks are born historians. Every island, every family has
a chronicle but few are better served than Oinoussai which
owes its name to the vines it grew – *oinos* is Greek for wine –
and was first mentioned by Herodotus and St. Luke. Family
records bring to life the turbulent past of clashes between east
and west, Islam and Christendom.

Past and present merge. There's the village of Castro –
Italian for fortress – dating back to Genoese seafarers of the
middle ages who turned Oinoussai into a naval observation
post and built a fortress where the village now stands. The
Genoese were driven out by the Turks and all they left behind
were a few coins buried in the ground and a few superstitions –
a Genoese Friar still stalks Oinoussai as a ghost. To the Turks
it was *Koyun Adasi* (Sheep's Island) – they gave it to Admiral
Mustapha (Fingerless) Pasha from whom it passed into the
hands of the Islamic religious authorities.

Oinoussians still talk of their forefather's futile struggle to
get title deeds to their land, the extortionate tribute the Turks
extracted from them and the delegations they sent to Constantinople to plead for reasonable treatment. They dropped
petitions into the path of the Sultan which was protocol.
They did not get very far – at one stage three Oinoussian
elders were kept in prison for three years for refusing to pay
up.

In these areas of mixed-up religions and nationalities the
settlers who came from Kardamila in 1700 A.D. were Greeks
of Turkish nationality, Christians in a Mohammedan country.
They built their first church in 1775 because in winter the sea
was too rough to take the bodies of the dead to Kardamila for
religious burial. The fifty families of Oinoussai 'tilled even the
rocks' to wrest a living from the inhospitable soil. They were
as inhospitable as their island and stopped more people coming
in to compete for the meagre spoils. Not content to remain
shepherds, their sons crossed to Chios to sign on with ships

which served Turkish trade but were almost exclusively manned by Greeks.

Overnight these ships became men-of-war when the Greeks rose against the Turks in the War of Liberation of 1821. Fearful actrocities were committed on both sides but this was the birth of the Greek fleet which rose from a sea of blood . . .

As we stood in the little harbour of Oinoussai an islander pointed out the spot where Greek ships, some hundred and fifty years ago, patrolled the shores when a Turkish convoy sailed across their path. The Greeks pounced, pillaged the Turkish ships and massacred crews and passengers, among them a Turkish judge who was taking the Sultan's present to Mecca, or it may have been a religious leader with his harem, his children and his retinue. There were no survivors. In retaliation the Turks hanged the Greek Orthodox Patriarch but the Greek version is that he was martyred long before the incident.

Turkish atrocities were on an even bigger scale. A famous painting by Eugene Delacroix, the French nineteenth century romantic, depicts *The Massacre of Chios in March* 1822 when all but 1,800 of the 30,000 Greek Christians of Chios were slain, sold into slavery or scattered. Oinoussai suffered along with Chios and the few survivors fled to the island of Syros.

For eight years Oinoussai was left deserted before the Turks allowed the islanders to return. They picked up the threads of their lives and rebuilt their community. The young men went to sea, saved and dreamed of owning their own ships. Their dreams may not have come true for a long time had it not been for the Crimean War which, as every war ever since, brought a big boom in shipping. By the time it ended in 1856, only twelve families remained to tend their flocks. Every able-bodied Oinoussian, man and boy, was at sea.

With a little money in their pockets, the sailors returning from the wars turned their dream into reality. They commissioned their first boats in Chios, whose little shipyard was to them what Sparrow Point is to American shipowners. But soon they decided to build on their own island, imported timber, engaged a master boat-builder, a few skilled shipwrights and a

34

blacksmith. They still had to go to Chios for masts, sails, rope – and credit. Launching their craft with makeshift sails they took them to Chios where brokers advanced money more readily when they saw the ships in their own harbour. Slowly Oinoussai was getting a respectable fleet together.

1856 was also the year Konstantine J. Pateras was born. Much of what we know about the origin of the vast Oinoussian shipping fortunes comes from his autobiography which his grandson John A. Hadjipateras has lovingly reproduced in a slim leather-bound volume, and on which another Oinoussian, Andrea G. Lemos, drew for his massive history of Greek shipping. The life of Konstantine Pateras is the story of the Island of the Rich and more than that – it traces the history of the fabulous Greeks to its very beginning and shows how one ship led to another until they grew into multi-million ton fleets.

The son of John C. Pateras, whose master's diploma entitled him to captain ships of the Turkish armada, Konstantine had three sisters (who soon complicated the family beyond analysis) and two younger brothers, Nicolas and Diamantis, whose descendants spread the name of Pateras far and wide and started shipping empires of their own which are still flourishing. At the age of seven he was sent to the little village school on Oinoussai and should have gone on to High School at Chios but dreaded the separation from his family. He had no fear of the sea, and rather than continue his education, went to sea with his father at the age of twelve, a hard and dangerous life with meagre rations, little respite and no pay at all. The family hoped he would go on to better things but three voyages later John Pateras contracted dysentery and died leaving Konstantine, his other children and his widow to fend for themselves.

In his will, attested by a notary, he settled his 'entire movable and immovable property' on his wife asking her to pay his debts, whether incurred at sea or on shore, if they were proven with or without promissary notes. Should she remarry she was to have her dowry back and the field with the fig trees near a place called Stenaka. John Pateras left fifty

Turkish gold pounds to his two elder daughters and asked that his youngest be given the dowry he still owed her.

'Being the eldest,' young Konstantine noted with a typically Greek sense of family responsibility, "I had to continue as a seaman because I had to be on board the vessel our father left us, and because rearing sheep and goats and cultivating the land could not provide us with a livelihood.' Already a shipowner in the making, the twelve year old with only the most elementary schooling prepared a list of Oinoussai's thirty sailing boats, half a dozen of them belonging to members of the Pateras clan, as many to Lemos families, to their relatives, to Lyras and several others.

An older relative was put in charge of the vessel John Pateras had left behind but after three years all he had to show for it were losses and damage to the ship. She was sold for 500 Turkish gold pounds, 300 of which the widow Pateras invested in a 150 ton sailing ship built on Syros. Her two sons-in-law, both members of the Lemos family and partners in the venture, struggled on for another seven years. Still the ship would not yield much more than the barest necessities for her owners.

Only God knows how Konstantine managed to save eighty Turkish gold pounds by the time he was twenty-two, enough to get him his first ship or at least part of a ship. In January 1879, his savings plus another sixty pounds which he borrowed, bought him a half share in a 120 ton vessel belonging to another Lemos. The *Evangelistria* was the first of the many ships which make up the various Pateras fleets. Konstantine carried timber and charcoal on his own account and sold it to other islands and in Asia Minor. Able shipowners could already make their fortunes quickly. Within a year he had paid his debt and still had thirty-five pounds in hand. Another year, and he could afford to build a house for himself.

Again tragedy struck Chios. The earthquake of 1881 ravaged the island and destroyed many buildings. In bitter cold people slept in the open until wealthy compatriots living abroad sent blankets, timber and money. Among Oinoussians who came to their aid were Michael K. Lemos, great-grandfather of the great Costa, and John Pateras, great-grandfather of John A. Hadjipateras on his mother's side. Quakes were still rocking Chios when the two men, having taken gifts of food and timber to Chios in their caique, set out on their return voyage. A sharp northerly wind was blowing, another ship with full sails rammed the caique which capsized. Lemos and Pateras managed to jump clear but were dragged down by their heavy clothes and drowned. Their bodies were picked up and taken to Oinoussai where they lie buried.

In Oinoussai – and in Chios – Konstantine Pateras was already one of the leading citizens. Now that his house was completed in the traditional island style he was no longer content to spend his free evenings with the island's other young men endlessly talking in the coffee-house next door to the small shop and watching the donkeys carting water from the wells or wandering down to the wooden jetty harbour which was the hub of Oinoussai's island existence.

Konstantine was looking for a wife. He did not have to look far. The handsome young Katingo Pateras on whom his roving eye came to rest, was a relative – there were few girls on the island to whom he was not related – one of the four daughters of George Pateras, Oinoussai's finest and wealthiest sailor. She accepted Konstantine and received a big dowry. Katingo's father was proud to have married off his five daughters so well. Five daughters? He only had four but gave one of them two dowries which in his arithmetic made it five.

Katingo bore Konstantine five children all of whom were equally well launched into married life. Daughter Irene's husband was another Pateras (George), the eldest boy John took a Lyras girl as his wife and a younger son, Adamantios, married Rallia Pateras, Nicolas married the daughter of wealthy Piraeus banker and Mayor Panayotopoulos, and Maria, the youngest, an offspring of the wealthy Fafalios shipping family from Chios.

On the treacherous seas, it was not all smooth sailing. Six years after Konstantine Pateras acquired the *Evangelistria*, she was wrecked in a storm and went down with her cargo, a grievous loss because neither ship nor cargo was insured. All Captain Pateras had left was three-hundred Turkish pounds. He and brothers Nicolas and Diamantis put their heads together and decided to buy a 220 ton schooner, *Dimitrios* which they worked for three years as partners carrying freight on charter until they had earned enough to exchange her for a bigger vessel, Konstantine controlling fifty per cent and his brothers sharing the other fifty.

They were haunted by the fate of the *Evangelistria*. What if the *Dimitrios*, too, went down uninsured? They could not survive another disaster but there was no easy way out. Though Oinoussai was already an important maritime centre, the money market was still in Chios, and Chios brokers would not insure Oinoussian vessels at their full value. Rather than accept lower valuations many Oinoussain ships like the *Evangelistra*, sailed without insurance cover, an early instance of the insurance problems that plagued the Greeks right into the nineteen-fifties.

For Konstantine and his fellow islanders there was only one solution – to start their own insurance company. They joined forces, fixed premiums, covered their own ships and recruited clients. Many owners of small vessels preferred the new insurance company to established Chios brokers who had ruled the roost for so long. The Chiots tried to lure them back into their net, but they had missed the boat – and a lot of business.

How proud Konstantine and his associates were! It was only a few years since they had scraped a few pounds together to buy their first ship. Now they were in insurance: 'Imagine what treasure we uneducated men left to our island,' Konstantine wrote. The new Marine Insurance Company gave Oinoussai prestige and kept the island's merchant fleet intact. So well trusted were the self-made brokers, they had only to tell an owner 'You are insured' and he accepted their word without waiting for the contract. Konstantine Pateras was the company's first chairman and treasurer.

In 1884, he took time off to travel to Jerusalem to pay his devotions at the Holy Sepulchre. Like Muslim pilgrims visiting Mecca, he (not his brothers) added the prefix Hadji to his name and became known as Hadjipateras, but, Hadji or Pateras, it was still the same family. Greeks under Turkish rule, though jealous of their national identity, adopted many customs from their overlords but Oinoussian ships were registered in Greek ports and their sailors thought of themselves as Greeks. The Turks did not mind – Oinoussai was such an insignificant little island.

The turn of the century – and smoke rising from the sea signalled a problem and an opportunity. The steamship arrived on the Greek scene. Oinoussian sailing vessels could not compare with the new-fangled ships. But how to raise the big capital needed to buy the modern vessels? No Oinoussian captain could do it on his own, and after much heart searching Konstantine Hadjipateras decided to pool his resources with two others, a Pateras and a Lemos. This is how most of the great Greek shipping partnerships began.

One proud exhibit in the Oinoussai Museum is a picture of the 3,550 ton steamship *Marietta Ralli*, memento of a love affair between a captain and a ship and a turning point in the island's history. She was only a vague thought in Konstantine's mind in May 1905 when he travelled to Constantinople, capital of shipping in his part of the world. He was like a man from out of town looking for a bride in the big city and when he set eyes on the thirteen year old girl in Constantinople Harbour it was love at first sight.

She was a fine looking ship with a gleaming hull. He looked her over as any suitor might, studied her history, inspected every nook and cranny and went down to the engine room to make himself familiar with the complicated machinery. The asking price was 13,300 Turkish pounds, just about as much as he and his two partners could raise. They bought her outright – the first steamship to come under Oinoussian control. Did I not say, that, with the Greeks, one ship soon leads to another? A few voyages with profitable cargoes and Konstantine bought another steamer, the eighteen years old *Leandros* – 2,600 tons, cost 9,700 Turkish pounds – this time in partnership with

brothers Nicolas and Diamantis Pateras. He gave up the
Marietta Ralli to his original partners and concentrated on the
Leandros.

For him it was a big moment: 'Without wishing to boast',
he noted in his memoirs, 'I attribute our progress to certain
moral qualities, our energetic application, our efficiency, our
thrift, the austerity of our family life in Oinoussai and, let me
add, our inborn flair for business. Our progress seems all
the more remarkable for our obscurity. We were quite unknown to the outside world, quite without protection and had
neither capital nor education. That is why we feel proud of
ourselves.'

This was the secret formula of early Greek shipping to
which the big enterprises owe their origin. Greek shipowners
are no longer the hardy, thrifty islanders and intrepid captains
of yore but even in their silk suits, their luxury yachts, their
apartments in *Claridge's* or the *Plaza*, they keep the spirit of
their ancestors alive.

Leandros did so well that the brothers bought a second ship,
the *Archimedes* (age: twenty-two years, size: 3,400 tons, price:
8,700 Turkish pounds, half of it on loan from the Bank of
Athens). Who would not be a shipowner? Besides, there was
another war in the offing. The purchase was no sooner completed when the Balkans exploded. In the first of the two
Balkan wars (1912-1913) Greeks, Serbs and Bulgars fought the
Turks but not many months later the line-up switched aud
Bulgaria was the odd man out with Greeks, Serbs, Rumanians
and Turks fighting the new enemy.

Masters, engineers and sailors of Oinoussai, like Greeks
everywhere, enlisted to fight under the Greek flag. The Greek
Government, requisitioned the *Archimedes* and, when the
Leandros emerged from the Suez Canal after a long voyage,
claimed her too, while the *Marietta Ralli* (captain, Cristos
Lemos) carried Bulgarian prisoners from Salonika to Piraeus.
Chios was liberated from the Turkish régime and a Greek
warship sailed to Oinoussai where the captain hoisted the Greek
flag and took possession of the islands in the name of the King

of the Hellenes. Oinoussai's leader was Panayotis Lemos, an uncle of Costa M. Lemos.

Was it peace? It was not. By the time the Hadjipateras vessels were restored to their owners, the first world war was upon them. *S.S. Archimedes* was caught in the Black Sea and could not get out – there was nothing but to sell her to the Rumanians at a knock-down price. *Leandros*, like other Greek ships, joined the allies.

In Athens, Konstantine Hadjipateras contemplated his position. He and his brothers had large families, no fewer than seventeen children between them. If they were to get a proper education and a share in the business, the *Leandros* alone could not support them. His solution was to buy another ship.

It was, Konstantine Hadijpateras recalled, 'a great problem, extremely difficult, not to say impossible'. You had to have your ears to the ground – or rather to the sea. Konstantine was all ears. He happened to be in Piraeus when he picked up a whisper that a good ship was coming on the market and quickly made his bid. The vessel he bought was called *Sappho*, age twenty-five years, cost 20,600 Turkish pounds. He took delivery of her in 1916, retained a sixty per cent share for himself and gave each of his brothers twenty per cent. Between them *Sappho* and *Leandros* were quite capable of solving the family's financial problems.

But not for long. Carrying coal from Cardiff to Lisbon in August 1916, *Leandros* was steaming past Barcelona when a German U-boat surfaced, ordered the crew to take to the boats and blasted her out of the sea. Being under-insured, naturally, her loss, including loss of earnings, set Konstantine back some 50,000 Turkish pounds. Four months later, *Sappho* shared her sister ship's fate. She too was torpedoed. Though better insured, her loss was a disaster to the family. When the insurance company paid up a year or so later, the three brothers collected all outstanding monies and dissolved the partnership. Konstantine was left with 90,000 Turkish pounds for himself and his sons. His two brothers shared 43,000 Turkish pounds.

The proliferation of the Pateras-Hadjipateras family was such that it is almost beyond one's wits to follow them all. Konstantine's son Adamantios, as astute as his father, snapped up a ship in Piraeus for 10,000 Turkish pounds and sold her at twice the price, his brothers and uncles sharing in the profit. There were few other opportunities of his kind.

Each of the brothers, Konstantine, Nicolas and Diamantis set up a firm of his own, each with his own sons, a pattern followed by all traditional Greek shipping families – once the new generation is old enough to join the business, the fathers separate their interest. It is a constant process. Like the Hydra they grow more and more heads, launch more and more firms – ships, that is – which multiply.

A few years after the war, Konstantine and his sons resumed their shipping activity. By 1923 they were again investing in new ships. The hard core of their fleet were the 8,000 ton *Aghios Nicolaos*, named after the patron saint of sailors – they were never without a ship of that name – the 11,000 ton *Konstantinos Hadjipateras*, one of the biggest ships of the Greek fleet in the thirties, and the 7,000 ton *Katingo Hadjipateras*, built in Sunderland in 1910. They were happy ships but the crews complained because they had to paint such long names on bows and sterns.

For Konstantine himself it was back to Oinoussai to build – not ships but a church. A new church was needed in place of the old St Nicola Church which was crumbling away and Konstantine threw himself into the project with the same application he devoted to his shipping coups. The Pateras and Lemos families raised 2,700 Turkish pounds and every Oinoussian made a contribution. A splendid new church was consecrated in 1928. The families built new and bigger houses, roads, public utilities, schools and a monument to the 'Unknown Teacher', the only one I have seen anywhere in the world. They could not do enough for their island.

All went well until the Italians attacked Albania and the second world war cast its shadow ahead. Oinoussian ships were put on war footing, able-bodied islanders joined the Greek

Navy. In May 1941 it was the turn of Greece. The Germans invaded the island of Crete from the air which had never before been attempted. A Lemos ship was bombed by the Luftwaffe and the captain killed. Greece could not long resist the onslaught of the Wehrmacht and the German writ spread to the Aegean islands. When little Oinoussai was occupied it was like a sentence of slow strangulation.

Still largely barren and entirely dependent on outside supplies, the island ran out of food and was faced with starvation. Remittances from serving sailors, sole income of almost every family, ceased to arrive. The Germans threw people out of their homes and requisitioned household utensils, bedding and whatever took their fancy. They imposed a strict curfew. Nobody was allowed to leave the island – even the short crossing to Chios required a special permit. Being a long way from home, the Nazi troops were frightened, jumpy and unpredictable. Miltiades Lemos, the island's new leader, was at his wits end.

Older people were hardest hit. Michael C. Lemos, waiting for his son Costa to come to his rescue, was one of many who did not survive the German occupation. Maria Diamanteras whose husband served with the British Navy was arrested, and so were his brothers. An islander who was found with a gun was sent to a concentration camp in Germany, never returned, and is presumed to have died in captivity. Every other week somebody was imprisoned for one offence or another.

Two islanders who were taken to Mitiline on Lesbos for questioning, turned the tables on the German guards, abducted them and escaped. In retaliation Pantelis Pateras and his wife, Constantine, George and Andreas Lemos, Peter Pateras and several others were arrested. When German soldiers contracted a venereal disease, the physician, Dr Lemos was accused of sabotaging the German army. As tension grew between the islanders and their Nazi overlords, the German garrison commander asked for hostages for the good behaviour of Oinoussai. Mayor Miltiades Lemos and other elders, several Lemos and Pateras among them, volunteered and went into captivity.

It was not a one way traffic into German prisons. Because of its proximity to the Turkish coast, Oinoussai was an ideal jumping board for Greeks trying to escape from their occupied country. Among those who made it was the tall, young Marcos D. Lemos who already had a reputation for doing things faster than most. His Oinoussian villa, called *Strovili* after the nearby rock, was built in a record time of three months. Strovili Lemos, as he was known (there are so many Marcos Lemos that they can only be told apart by their nicknames), escaped from Oinoussai in a rowing boat, reached Turkey and went on to Egypt where he joined the Greek Air Force.

Grave as the situation of the islanders was, their ships fared even worse. The havoc started in October 1939 when World War Two was only a little over a month old and Greece not as yet combatant. Carrying a cargo of timber from Alaska to Britain, the *Katingo Hadjipateras*, with Captain Costis Lemos and a crew of twenty-five, was off Denmark on the last stage of her voyage when she ran into a German minefield, was struck and crippled. She was salvaged and taken into Copenhagen for repairs.

The first Greek ship to suffer in the war, she was a sensation while lying in her sick berth and could have made a lot of money had Captain Lemos charged a fee to the thousands of visitors who came to look at her. She rejoined the allied merchant navy, resumed her career and made another thirty trips across the Atlantic carrying food supplied from Canada to Britain, the only Hadjipateras ship to survive the war: 'It was miraculous,' said John Hadjipateras. Still proud and strong when the war ended, she continued for another five years until she returned to Sunderland to be broken up where she was born. In his apartment in Regent's Park, London, where he is surrounded by mementoes of the family's shipping history, John keeps the St Nicolas Ikon she carried on all her voyages.

Nothing was saved from the *Konstantinos Hadjipateras* which was lost off the English coast, nor from the *Aghios Nicolaos* which sailed with a cargo of iron ore from West Africa to

Britain in 1941 and nearly made it, but not quite. Off the coast of Portugal she was stopped by a German U-boat whose commander ordered the crew into the lifeboats – all except Captain Elias Halkias who was made a prisoner of war. As the survivors made for Portugal the U-boat's guns put paid to the *Aghios Nicolaos*. Captain Halkias was carried away to Germany. A great character, *bon viveur* and enthusiastic gambler, he survived the war, returned to Greece and lived into his sixties.

Every Greek ship afloat was committed to the allies, serving under British auspices. Their owners were no longer in control. The British Ministry of Transport fixed the scale of payment according to tonnage, age and classification of the ships. Profits were strictly controlled. Greek shipowners are at pains to deny that their shattering war losses entitled them to exorbitant compensation from the insurance companies. Some of them may well be right but others made up for years of under-insurance by pocketing compensation which was – shall we say? – not ungenerous.

It was a frustrating business for the Greeks to stand by power-less while their ships went down like ninepins until virtually none were left. Shipowners from Chios, Andros, Cephalonia, Ithaca, Crete, from all Greek islands shared the fate of the Oinoussians. With movement and opportunity restricted in war-time Britain, the 'London Greeks' moved on to the United States and became the 'New York Greeks'. Others, though their thoughts were with their ships were stranded inside Greece whether they liked it or not.

Konstantine Hadjipateras' sons and grandsons were with him in Greece until he died in Athens in 1943 at the ripe old age of eighty-seven. He had done his share for Oinoussai. Now it was the turn of his offspring.

Clandestine reports reaching Athens told of the island's tragedy. What could they do to help? With other descendants of Oinoussai, they devised a scheme to alleviate the suffering. It was no simple matter. Conditions in Athens were difficult, money was scarce, Greek currency almost worthless. The only way was to borrow against promissory notes to be repaid in English currency after the war. With the money they bought supplies and sent them to Oinoussai. A food distribution centre doled out rations but there was only enough for half the population. In Athens, the younger Oinoussians did not knuckle under the whip of the German occupation. John A. Hadjipateras, Adamantios' younger son, was one of the students active in the Greek resistance and risked his life editing and publishing an underground journal.

In July 1944 the shadow lifted. The Germans left Oinoussai but one of their units stayed on in Chios until September. Civil war raging on the mainland spread to the islands. Oinoussians took up arms, fought as guerrillas. Sniping developed into open battles. Several islanders were killed, some were captured and executed, quite a few abducted behind the Iron Curtain never to be heard of again. It was only in 1945 that, as Andrea G. Lemos put it, 'Oinoussai returned to the calm of our nation's freedom.'

For the shipowners it was back to work to start rebuilding their fleets. In 1946 they flocked to the United States where the American Government launched a rescue operation for European shipping (of which we shall hear more later). The Greeks were allocated a hundred Liberty ships to replace their staggering war losses.

The Oinoussians bagged twelve of them. Four went to the various branches of the Lemos family while the names of Pateras and Hadjipateras figured on the list with eight ships. Faithful to tradition, Hadjipateras Brothers named the first of their new vessels *Aghios Nicolaos* and the second *K.* (for Konstantine) *Hadjipateras*. The other six were shared by the firm of Nicolas and Diamantis Pateras which their sons took over.

While remaining tied to Oinoussai by their umbilical cords, the Oinoussians dispersed all over the world but did not exactly settle down. Like Costa M. Lemos, if not quite on such a grand scale, they established their offices in New York and London as well as in Athens, but their firms were mostly registered in tax havens of Central American 'flags of convenience' countries. However many ships an owner accumulated, each was run by a separate company so as to restrict liability.

The owners themselves moved from capital to capital, the original jet-setters, the world's most prosperous gipsies, pitching their expensive tents wherever their fancy guided them. Some took to their yachts paying tribute only to Neptune, others became coveted customers of luxury hotels maintaining permanent suites in several cities. They bought homes in the U.S., England, France, Switzerland and Greece.

Let me trace a few of them who I can almost see with the naked eye from where I sit in my London home. There is Marcos Lyras's splendid mansion, not much more than a stone's throw away in Avenue Road which is straddled with the houses of some of England's wealthiest families. His brother Costa Lyras keeps a residence on the northern fringe of Hyde Park and a splendid country house, Ripley Grange, in Essex. There are at least six branches of the Lyras family constantly producing boys, girls and ships. The emblem on the attractive funnels of the Lyras ships – funnels, as Onassis is fond of saying, are to ships what Easter bonnets are to ladies – is a lyra which is an ancient Greek harp but also (with a little latitude in spelling) stands for Lira, Greek for pound sterling, of which they have a few million.

There is Strovili Lemos, who, after leaving the Greek Air Force completed his education in Athens, learned his trade the hard way on family ships, married the very beautiful Chrysanthi Pateras and gave his London shipping company a name with an authentic Oinoussian ring, Lemos & Pateras. In the early fifties, when he decided to build himself a house in Winnington Road, the Millionaires' Row of North London, the £75,000 project provided for seven canopied bedrooms, five marble bathrooms, a chapel and a swimming pool in the grounds in the shape of Oinoussai Island – and two nurseries, one for a boy, one for a girl. Strovili and Chrysanthi had a twenty months old boy Dimitri but before the house was completed, Chrysanthi gave birth to a baby girl who was christened Kalliope. The name of the house – *Strovili*.

Strovili runs a fast yacht (*Strovili* of course), fast cars and fast horses. The stables at Warren Hill House, his Newmarket estate, are among the finest in England for training and breeding, and his most successful horse, Petingo, though no longer in training, won many races and challenged the great *Sir Ivor* for the 1968 'Two Thousand Guineas'.

Other members of the Lemos clan, in the meantime, were building ships. Strovili's cousins, the sons of Diamantis Lemos, a sea captain who started with only a few shares in ships, now have a fleet of some twenty tankers including the 80,000 *Captain Diamantis*, built in Japan in 1971 and named after their father. One member of the Lemos family, the venerable Andrea G. Lemos, stayed behind in Athens, was twice Mayor of Chios, and member of the pre-Junta Greek parliament and has produced as many learned tomes as ships. His wife Maria is a member of a Chios shipping family.

The Lemos family tree has sprouted many wondrous blooms, none brighter than George Christos Lemos whose ambition was to become a bishop ('The inclination has never passed') qualified as a lawyer instead but was inevitably lured back to the sea which is his tribe's natural habitat: 'All my friends were sailors,' George recalled to explain his conversion.

Now in his early seventies, a serene, wise, highly respected shipowner in semi-retirement, he holds court at the *Lausanne Palace*, the famous hotel by the Lac Leman, which attracts Greek shipowners in prodigious numbers. Looking back on his long career he said: 'In 1928 I left the legal profession and acquired my first ships. I bought a 7,000 ton cargo ship, *Triana*, which means Trident, sold it after a few years and replaced it with another vessel, *Efploia*, which is Greek for Fair Sailing . . .'

It has been fair sailing for George Lemos ever since. Business expanded, more ships joined his fleet which he controlled from shipping offices in London and New York in association with another Lemos and a Pateras. Shipping organisations conferred honours and offices on him but the philosopher which lurks in so many Greeks would not be denied. George Lemos devoted all his spare energies to spiritual matters. One of his endeavours took concrete shape in the *Movement for Solidarity*: 'We open our arms to humanity and global solidarity', is how he describes his aims. The *Movement* was acclaimed by many public figures, presidents Kennedy and de Gaulle among them.

Still a bishop at heart, George Christos Lemos took an active interest in the ecumenical movement and, in 1971, visited Rome as a member of the Greek Orthodox Church delegation. He was received in audience by the Pope who conferred on him the honour of a Commandant of the Order of Pope Gregorius.

'Will you permit me to pin this decoration on you with my own hands?' the Holy Father asked.

'The honour is great,' George Christos Lemos replied, 'the man is small. The graces of the churches of Christ are also great. I thankfully accept this honour. It is not you or me – it is the Grace of God.'

Through family, friendship and business ties, George Lemos remains closely linked with the Oinoussians. At the *Lausanne Palace*, he is always surrounded by members of the younger generation of Pateras and Hadjipateras, two clans which early ventured forth from Oinoussai to the Greek mainland and hence to western Europe. Adamantios K. Hadjipateras settled in Switzerland where his daughter Katingo married Minos Colocotronis, a Cretan with Peloponnese antecedents, whose sensational rise in the shipping world is the subject of a later chapter. From Switzerland Adamantios moved to Paris where his sons, Costa and John, were both married in the early fifties: Costa to Tika Pateras – he has seven children, seven more shipowners in the making; and John to the delicately beautiful Maro Pateras.

The two couples are typical of the intricate Greek marriage game which is as difficult to analyse as the backgammon contests with which shipowners love to while away their time. Intermarriage, so common among Greek islanders, has the advantage that the generous dowries, mostly ships and share in ships, remain in the family or at least within the orbit of the native island. It produces strange patterns. In the passage of time, Maro Hadjipateras' younger sister married a son of her husband's elder brother which makes John his nephew's brother-in-law and Maro her sister's aunt.

When he finally made London his home, Adamantios K. Hadjipateras, with a Greek shipowner's predilection for luxury hotels, installed himself in a permanent suite at the *Grosvenor House* in Park Lane where his big family gathers around him in the lounge on many an evening for coffee and talk *a la recherche du temps perdu*. Pateras everywhere – the dazzling Mitsa Pateras, granddaughter of Nicolas, married George Dracoulis whose name is synonymous with his native island of Ithaca.

The younger generation has come a long way from the rough and tough life of the early Oinoussians who were more adept at reading the stars than the printed word. A new-style owner, John A. Hadjipateras mixes shipping with literary work and public service. His hobby is *Krikos* (Link), a journal which links Greeks at home and in *xenitia* – I suspect it costs him a fair amount of money. While his older brother Costa holds the fort of their shipping business ('Were it not for him I could not pursue my outside interests'), John represents Greek shipping at international congresses, a division of duties which is not uncommon.

The bigger their fleet and their fortune, the more reticent Greek shipowners are about them but Oinoussians are proud of the island's wealth because it is so widely spread. There are at least fifty Oinoussian families who are each worth more than a million, pound sterling rather than dollars, not bad for an island with a population of 1,580. Their little Golden Book lists over a hundred Oinoussians in London alone, eleven Hadjipateras, twenty-two Pateras and thirty-three Lemos among them. A pre-war chart of Oinoussian shipping shows twenty-seven funnels, each representing a shipping line. In the post-war charts, the number has risen to forty-seven.

The owners who belong to the aristocracy of Greek shipping are as jealous of their tradition and island heritage as any belted earl of his embattled royal ancestors. Each of their shipping coups means another windfall for Oinoussai – and let no one quote the old hexameter about Greeks carrying gifts. Only one gift gained a brief international notoriety. Indeed, Oinoussai may not have emerged from its anonymity, had it not been for the forbidding, fortress-like Convent of Evangelismos which looks out of character even in such a God-fearing community. Visitors are not encouraged and few are allowed past the gates. The islanders who proudly show off the sights of Oinoussai to the occasional stranger do not like to dwell on the subject.

The Convent, Oinoussai's most expensive edifice, was built by Katingo Pateras, sister of the very worldly Strovili Lemos, at a cost of one million dollars of her shipping fortune. She is one of the ten nuns who inhabit it. Among Greek Christians there is nothing unusual about private individuals financing religious institutions or about prominent women taking the veil – the late Princess Alice, mother of the Duke of Edinburgh and mother-in-law of the Queen established her own order of working nuns in Greece.

For years Katingo Pateras and the other nuns of Oinoussai pursued their prayers in obscurity and seclusion behind the walls of their convent until, in the early sixties, a small diplomatic rumpus between Greece and the United States propelled them into the headlines. The central figure of the affair was a fresh-faced twenty-three year old girl from Seattle, Christine Coryell, who was converted to the Greek Orthodox faith while studying at the University of Washington – and disappeared. Relatives eventually traced her to the Convent of Evangelismos. Like some families in similar circumstances, they were reluctant to give her up to her new-found vocation.

Christine's uncle, a football coach at San Diego State College, screamed blue murder – or, at any rate, abduction! His niece had come under the hypnotic spell of Abbess Pateras, he proclaimed – Katingo was not the Abbess and had only recently entered the convent. Some terrible things were supposed to be going on there. Christine's father went to Oinoussai to persuade her to return to the States: 'I am here of my own free will,' she told him. She had long been thinking of taking the veil, she said, had visited the convent and decided to stay: 'I am happy with monastic life,' was her final word. The American authorities were consulted and there were diplomatic exchanges before the storm subsided. Since then the outside world has seen and heard nothing of Katingo Pateras and the nuns of Oinoussai.

Other girls come to the island, though not to be wedded to God. Descendants of Oinoussai, the locals will tell you, come on their second honeymoon, their second holiday and for their second burial. Or to become engaged. Irini, the handsome daughter of 'Captain A' Mavrophillipas, returned in August 1969 to get her engagement ring from Marcos Christos Lemos, yet another union of two old island families. Half the population joined in the celebrations at the Nautical Club which is Oinoussai's social centre.

At the same club, the late King Paul and Queen Frederika of Greece once danced with the local elite. Photographs on the walls commemorate the visit of the royal couple who came to pay tribute to the cradle of Greek shipping which will never lie fallow. The future of Oinoussai is anchored in the Captain's School where a brisk young naval officer, Lieutenant Michael Dorkofikis, trains the island's youngsters to take over from the old-timers. Every one of these boys nurses a dream in which he sees himself, if not as another Costa M. Lemos, then certainly on the bridge of the first million ton tanker whose captain, surely, must be a Greek – and a Greek from Oinoussai.

Training goes on throughout the winter when storms sweep the island and whip up the sea around it. Come summertime and the islanders welcome their wealthy relatives ashore. Leaving their mansions, country estates and counting houses in the western world behind, members of Oinoussai's millionaire families converge on their native rocks to swim, sail, talk, pray for a few glorious weeks, and walk in the footsteps of their forefathers.

Among them without fail is John A. Hadjipateras, who,

with his wife and teenage daughters, moves into the house his grandfather Konstantine built almost a century ago. Another century and his grandchildren will take their children on the same annual pilgrimage, and so will the descendants of the Lemos, Lyras, Mavrophillipas and all other Oinoussian families. Their undying devotion, generation after generation, is the real wealth of the Island of the Rich.

IV

GREEK SHIPPING'S TRUE BLUE HUE

ANCIENT motorcars navigate narrow, dusty streets and
pull up at splendid villas whose caretakers peer
through high windows forever awaiting a visit from
absentee owners. Kardamila is a charming, simple, unaffected
village, a miniature city really, on the north-eastern fringe of
the island of Chios.

Chios is not short of status symbols. Homer was probably
born on the island, Christopher Columbus sailed in long before
he discovered the other place. Thirty-eight of the hundred and
forty premier Greek shipping families hail from Chios which
has honoured them with statues and street names. Kardamila's
main share in the shipping bonanza is one big name – Livanos –
which appeared in the annals of an historic English house,
when Tina Livanos married the Marquess of Blandford, son and
heir of the Duke of Marlborough and kinsman of Winston
Churchill. Shades of European land battles to match the naval
exploits of the Greeks even though the battles turned out to be
domestic rather than heroic . . .

It is only rarely that the patience of the staff at the Livanos
villa is rewarded as happened in the summer of 1971 when a
helicopter descended on Kardamila and disgorged a handsome dark young man whose natural habitat is the chief
executive's suite of his offices in Athens, London and New
York. For the remote and becalmed village it was a spectacular
occasion. The local notables turned out in strength to welcome
George S. Livanos, head of the shipping group which bears
his name, to the island of his ancestors.

Born in New York some thirty-six years ago, the young
Greek tycoon came on a traditional family mission – to
inaugurate Kardamila's new girls' school built with some

£70,000 of his shipping fortune. Standing under the bust of his grandfather (George Livanos, 1854-1925), George, essentially a private man of few words, addressed the girls with a few crisp sentences. It was a brief ceremony.

A walk through the old Aegean village, a quick visit to the Livanos villa, a public reception, and he was on his way back to Piraeus for a few days before resuming his unending round of the world's capitals. The school was only the latest instalment in a veritable orgy of modernisation projects – roads, water systems, street lighting – financed by Greek shipowners from Chios. Chief beneficiaries, apart from Kardamila, are the two hundred and fifty families of the tiny village of Armolia who never shared the wanderlust of their fellow islanders or joined the sailors' exodus from which other villages reap their harvest of remittances.

Quickly as the Livanos presence passed, it stirred memories. Few villagers remember George's grandfather but they speak frequently and affectionately of his father, Stavros G. Livanos, one of the great characters of the island race. With a twinkle in their eyes, they conjure up the image of the gruff little sea captain with the thick dark hair and the aggressive moustache whose wealth never mellowed nor changed the attitudes of a lifetime. Taciturn and secretive, the only subject which turned him on was the memory of his early days at sea. He loved to talk about the time when he and his brother, both still in their teens, sailed with their father on a ship called *Evangelistria*, same name as John Pateras' vessel. Whenever his shipping friends discussed multi-million dollar deals, he harped back to days when there was little to eat and every voyage a battle with death. More than once, he recalled, he was swept off the deck in rough seas and only narrowly escaped drowning. Such experiences make a man, he used to say.

He would not talk as freely about his early financial operations which enabled him to buy a ship of his own, then another and another. A man without outside interests, he never relaxed until, at the age of thirty-five, he met Arietta Zafikaris, the daughter of a rich Chios merchant, who was twenty years younger than he. He fell in love with her, the dowry was right, and they were married. Before long Livanos moved from Chios to Athens and from Athens to London, the route along which successful Greek shipowners sailed to the top of the charts. Their two daughters, Eugenie and Athina, were born in London but when Arietta Livanos expected her third child, Stavros was confident it would be a boy and made sure that he would qualify as an American citizen. He was right – George Livanos was born in New York in 1936.

By this time his father was already a very wealthy man and his fleet the biggest under Greek control. Genie and Tina went to an exclusive English girls' school. Their mother, a sleepy-eyed beauty, enjoyed London's social life but Stavros was completely wrapped up in his work: 'He lived for his ships and for his family – in that order,' Onassis once told me. Though he showered luxuries on his wife and daughters, he looked twice at every penny he spent on himself, travelled to the City by underground, munched chestnuts bought in six-penny packets from a street vendor, and queued behind clerks and typists at cheap lunch counters for a sandwich and a cup of coffee. Evenings, his recreation was a game of bridge with modest stakes.

Like other Greek shipowners, Stavros Livanos left London when the war made it difficult to conduct operations from the British Isles, and after a short stay in Canada settled in the United States. Home was a suite in New York's *Plaza Hotel*. The girls went to Miss Hewitt's Classes where their cosmopolitan upbringing received an American gloss; but they came to be more English than American and at heart remained more Greek than English. They were delightful but different, Genie, dark and sporting was more serious than the fair-haired Tina, a bright little butterfly, elegant even as a teenager, witty and full of fun. Though they acquired all the social graces, as Tina once told me, they never learned to cook anything more elaborate than a boiled egg.

At the *Plaza* 'Ari' Onassis, the up and coming newcomer to the shipping business, was among the Greeks who sat at the feet of Stavros Livanos. By far the youngest of the regular crowd, he caught the eye of the two demure Livanos girls who made their bow to their father's shipping friends. The more he saw of Tina, the more he liked her. She was not yet seventeen – he twenty-one years older – when he began to court her, followed her to Long Island, where Stavros Livanos had a house, and raced past her in a speed boat flying a flag with the letters T.I.L.Y. ('Tina I Love You') until she promised to marry him – father permitting. Stavros Livanos did not permit.

He did not disapprove of Onassis who, he thought, had a great future ahead of him. Nor could he reasonably object to the age difference which was the same that separated him and his wife. He simply expected Ari to ask for the hand of Eugenie, the elder daughter, which would have been quite in order: 'He looked upon his daughters as if they were ships', Ari said enjoying his own joke, 'and thought the first of the line should be the first to be disposed of.'

The account which Onassis gave me of his courtship, his engagement (Livanos finally consenting) and his marriage has been published in a dozen languages and re-told in books which have drawn liberally on my Onassis biography.

Presently a second younger-generation Greek appeared on the scene. Stavros Niarchos, Ari's hawk-nosed, debonair friend, three years younger than he, was laying siege to Genie Livanos. Papa Livanos who had just given his younger daughter away was as uncertain about Niarchos as he had been about Onassis.

What did they know about Eugenie's suitor? That Niarchos (whose name means 'shipmaster') was a mainland Greek whose father, a shopkeeper from the city of Sparta, had spent some years in *xenitia* in Philadelphia and Buffalo, New York, running a restaurant – Stavros' sister Mary was born in the U.S.A. – but returned to Greece where he did not do very well. That young Stavros went to work for his rich uncles, the Koumandaros brothers, who were grain merchants, that he persuaded them to buy their own ships to save on transport costs, and acquired a 60,000 dollar share in one of the ships when the uncles dissolved their partnership shortly before the second world war. That this ship was insured for a million dollars, and was bombed by the Luftwaffe in Antwerp Harbour early in the war, and that Niarchos bought a second ship and a third, climbing the steps of the insurance ladder as if to the Greek shipping manner born.

The record showed that Stavros Niarchos married a Greek Admiral's daughter in 1930 – a short-lived affair which ended in divorce – and eight years later took a second wife, a diplomat's widow. He led the good life in New York, joined the Greek Royal Navy, served as a naval attache in Washington, New York and Alexandria. Because he was frequently seen in the company of attractive women, it came as no surprise when he was divorced for a second time, but he provided handsomely for his ex-wife with whom he remained on friendly terms.

When he set his cap at the elder Livanos daughter, Ari Onassis was heard muttering that it was an unsuitable match. Niarchos was convinced that his erstwhile friend did not want him as a brother-in-law, and was bitterly resentful. It was the beginning of the most publicised family feud in modern times. Eugenie Livanos and Stavros Niarchos were married within the year. Like her sister, she received a handsome dowry. Tina's was an elegant New York town house in Sutton Square, Eugenie's was in cash. Papa Livanos also made down payments on two tankers, one for each of his sons-in-law but they had to take it from there.

Stavros and Eugenie moved into an apartment in Sutton Place, round the corner from Tina's house. Like everything Niarchos touched, it soon grew – first into a duplex, then into a triplex until he bought the whole house.

But there was no question of either Onassis or Niarchos getting their hands on the big Livanos fleet. For years to come, whenever the name of Livanos was mentioned in connection with Onassis and Niarchos, it was said that he was rich enough to buy out both of them; but the time was not far off when this was no longer true. Going their own way, except for a

few short-lived common ventures each of them amassed a
tanker fleet far bigger than that of their older, more conservative father-in-law. While Livanos paid cash for his ships, they
took advantage of sophisticated methods of finance and credit
to advance their fortunes. Both bought famous yachts, while
Stavros Livanos, like Costa M. Lemos, would not have a ship
that did not earn money.

On the way to their multi-million ton tanker fleet, both men
ran foul of the U.S. regulations governing the purchase of
American ships by foreigners, both were indicted, both
settled their disputes with the U.S. authorities but their common
troubles only aggravated their feud. Onassis who boldly flew
into the lion's den while under indictment and slugged it out
with the public prosecutor Warren Burger, now United States
Chief Justice, accused Niarchos of settling by abject surrender.
Both spoiled their wives, Niarchos scoring with bigger diamonds
and more expensive necklaces but the value of their gifts did
not differ by more than the odd million dollars.

After the 1939-45 war both transferred their headquarters
to Europe, Onassis establishing offices in Monte Carlo while
Niarchos installed his staff in two elegant Georgian town
houses in London's Mayfair. Onassis recruited his executives
largely from among Greek shipping families while Niarchos
engaged every aristocrat (two Yugoslav princelings among
them) who would follow his siren call and accept his extremely
generous remuneration.

The tastes of the brothers-in-law were as different as the
high powered, slightly ponderous yacht *Christina* in which
Onassis sailed into international society, and the sleek, three-
masted schooner *Creole*, the world's biggest sailing yacht, with
oak panelled cabins and Salvador Dali murals, which reflected
the personality of Stavros Niarchos. Ari's taste ran to bar stools
covered with the smooth skin of whales' testicles while Stavros
Niarchos collected old masters (with one fell swoop he bought
up Edward G. Robinson's collection of French Impressionists)
and took some of them with him on all his travels, hanging
them wherever he happened to stay for a few days.

The Livanos family life was complicated by the quarrels between Ari and Stavros Niarchos which grew angrier with the years as they competed for the best chateau on the Riviera, for the most eligible guests at their social events – when Winston Churchill honoured the Onassis yacht with his presence, Niarchos countered with a shipload of royalty – and trumped each other with even bigger tankers. Had it not been for their rivally, it might have taken much longer for tanker sizes to approach the million ton mark.

Unaffected by the manoeuvres of their hostile husbands, the Livanos sisters remained close throughout. Onassis and Niarchos might not be on speaking terms and call each other names in public, Genie and Tina spent as much time together as possible, mostly in St Moritz where they both enjoyed the wintersports, in Paris where they maintained big apartments or in London and New York. Like Odysseus sailing between Scylla and Charibdis, Stavros Livanos carefully navigated on a middle course. To visit Chios, he travelled by regular steamer from Athens except when Onassis gave him a lift in *Christina*, once with Winston Churchill, another time with Greta Garbo as fellow passengers. On Chios, he discarded the trappings of the rich shipowner and went out and about in a pair of jeans, a denim shirt, sandals and a straw hat to show that, a couple of hundred million dollars or no, he was still one of the boys.

In seaside cafés he rubbed shoulders with the tramps, scroungers and beggars of the island, spreading some of his wealth, if not always with great tact. Forgetting that even the poorest of his fellow islanders could be as obstinately independent as he was in his business dealings, he scattered sovereigns around him and exhorted the have-nots to pick them up. At least one of the derelicts was not tempted by the unexpected bounty, would not demean himself and bow before the great man. Greeks, high and low, dispense basic wisdom with the authority of ancient philosophers: 'The sea and the sky are the same colour for both of us,' the ragged but proud Chiot pronounced rejecting his rich compatriot's offerings. 'You and I will be covered by the same soil.'

Livanos was baffled. Sadly, he allowed the millionaire to take over, spending much of his time partridge and quail shooting in the south of the island, visiting churches and schools to whose upkeep he contributed with a charity as fiercely competitive as his shipping programme; other wealthy sons of Chios – Carras, Chandris, Fafalios, Halkias, Andreadis, Vassiliades and Xylas – were never far behind with their donations.

If there was anything his sons-in-law envied Stavros Livanos it was his island birth. A Greek shipowner without an island is like a king without his clothes and, in spite of their vast fortunes, the two land-lubbers Onassis and Niarchos felt positively naked. Niarchos was the first to do something about it and bought Spetsopoula Island, some 240 uninhabited acres in the Aegean, a helicopter's ride from Piraeus. He imported pheasants and partridges, and built a fifteen room villa and a dozen guest chalets with all the comforts of a metropolitan hotel.

In the same spirit, Onassis adopted Ithaca, the island of Odysseus, with an ardent possessive love and Ithaca reciprocated by making him an honorary citizen. It was not good enough. Since Ithaca was not for sale he started looking for the next best island in the Ionian Sea to buy and call his own. His search ended when he found Skorpios, an uninhabited islet off the west coast of Greece. The wild little rock with its neglected olive groves was going cheaply – the asking price was said to be no more than sixty thousand dollars.

Onassis snapped it up, including the even tinier Sparti Island next door so as to prevent neighbours from encroaching on his privacy. The new squire of Skorpios invested three million dollars to turn it into a flower-decked gem with six miles of roads and riding paths through the olive groves, a harbour for *Christina*, a villa, a dozen guest chalets with every mod. con., servants' quarters, stables, a telephone exchange and a pumping system, for the only thing which Ari could not conjure up on the island was water which has to be ferried across the sea from Lefkas every day. As he drove me around

Skorpios in his mini-moke, Onassis could not disguise his pride that he was the owner of an island at last.

Spetsopoula and Skorpios were part and parcel of the Niarchos-Onassis one-upmanship in the social sphere. They fought as bitterly to get the better of each other in business. Political in-fighting accompanied their rival bids for concessions – or rather monopolies – which were in the giving of the Greek Government. So as not to antagonise one or the other of the powerful combatants, Prime Minister Constantine Karamanlis handed down a Solomonic decision. Niarchos received a strip of coastline at Skaramanga near Athens where he built the impressive Hellenic Shipyards (giving a financial interest to Greek-born Princess Sophia, wife of the Spanish Pretender Juan Carlos) while Onassis was allocated control of the Greek national airline which he renamed Olympic Airways and has been running ever since. Even so, there were more valuable prizes to be picked up but the battle for those was not joined for another few years.

In the nineteen fifties, at least as far as Stavros Livanos knew, his daughters' marriages were running smoothly, and superficially they were. Tina and Ari spoilt their children who were both born in New York, Alexander in 1948 and Christina in 1950. That they were both American citizens by birth came in useful in the tanker dispute between their father and the U.S. Government which arose from the American ban on foreign ownership of American vessels and was settled by Onassis transferring the disputed ships to a twenty million dollar American shipping trust in the names of the children – it multiplied tenfold in value within a decade and was due to come under their direct control on Christina's twenty-first birthday in December 1971.

Alexander and Christina went to school in Paris and spent their holidays in Monte Carlo where their father owned a stake in the Casino, or on *Christina* where their nursery was a show place admired by all who saw it. Apart from the occasional crisis inevitable with a volatile character like Onassis, Tina seemed happy until 1959 when the friendship between Onassis and Maria Callas became public property and Tina walked out on her husband taking the children with her.

To old Stavros Livanos the break-up of his younger daughter's marriage came as a shock. Tina obtained a divorce in Alabama and was given custody of the children but said that she did not want any of Ari's money. She did not need it. Daughters of Greek shipowners were in the same league as the proverbial American heiresses of yore who linked their family fortunes with the titles of Europe's aristocracy.

With her marriage in ruins, Tina drew even closer to her sister who welcomed her into the Niarchos chalet in St. Moritz – wintersports was the favourite hobby of the Livanos girls. In personal and financial matters, it was natural that she should count on the advice of brother-in-law Stavros Niarchos – with Ari Onassis the common enemy, they were natural allies. Family ties grew into a deep friendship.

Still young, desirable, wealthy in her own right, it was a foregone conclusion that Tina would not remain unmarried for long. She had known the Marquess of Blandford for some time and, though belonging to vastly different worlds, by background and outlook, they were married in Paris in 1961. The romantic alliance of Kardamila and Blenheim Palace gave Greek shipping a true blue hue. The couple moved into Lee Place, next door to the palace on the Duke of Marlborough's estate in Oxfordshire and tried to lead an aristocratically discreet and unobtrusive life.

Tina never lost the jet habit of a lifetime and travelled around the world, visiting Paris where she maintained an apartment in the Avenue Gabriel overlooking the Elysée Palace Gardens, the South of France where the Blandfords rented a villa, St Moritz, where she stayed with Genie and Stavros Niarchos, New York and most frequently, Athens. Years after her divorce from Onassis she was still treated as the owner's privileged guests in the jets of her ex-husband's Olympic Airlines. In the passage of time, her daughter Christina rented an apartment in London's Mayfair not far from *Claridge's*, her father's favourite hotel. Tina often used the apartment as a *pied à terre* and, inevitably met Ari when he visited their daughter.

Unlike Onassis whose romance with Callas, mammoth rows with governments and big deals with oil companies (not to speak of his marriage to Jackie Kennedy when it came to pass) kept his name on the front pages and in the gossip columns, Stavros ('Onassis minus the personality') Niarchos managed to escape undue attention. Only when he and Genie entertained the ruling and non-ruling royalty of Europe were they caught in the headlines and Stavros Livanos heard his elder daughter described as 'a queen without a crown' or, less extravagantly but quite truthfully, as the most charming and natural lady of the international jet set.

Eugenie and Stavros Niarchos had four children – Philip, born in 1952, Spiros who came three years later, then Maria in 1958 and finally, in 1962, little Constantine, named after the present King of the Hellenes. The children shared their mother's dream life spending summer on Spetsopoula and winter in St Moritz where Niarchos' chalet compared with the czar's winter palace. New York, Athens, Paris, London (a permanent penthouse at *Claridge's*), a yacht, haute couture, exquisite jewellery: 'I am the happiest woman in the world,' Eugenie said. It was good for a father to know that his daughter was so content. Stavros Livanos did not live until Genie's dream-world ended in disaster.

In may 1963 he and his wife were at a hotel in Lausanne – occupying one room as usual, to avoid the expense of a suite – when he suffered a heart attack. A doctor ordered his immediate transfer to hospital, Genie, Tina and young George were summoned to his bedside but by the time they arrived the frugal millionaire sea captain was dead. A new breed of shipping tycoon took over – twenty-seven year old George S. Livanos, a stint at Oxford University, training in business administration and a spell as his father's aide at the Livanos offices in London behind him.

The fortune Stavros Livanos left behind was in the region of £100 million – accurate figures were difficult to obtain because

ABOVE This rare photograph shows the elite of Greek shipowners. When it was taken in Athens in 1970 these men controlled between them at least £500 million's worth of shipping. (Onassis, Niarchos and Livanos, absent from the assembly, control another £500 million's worth.) *Left to Right*: J. M. Carras (face partly hidden), C. M. Lemos, Prof. S. Andreadis (Shipowner and Banker), N. Kavounides, M. Colocotronis, J. Kulukundis, J. A. Hadjipateras, Prof. I. Holevas (the then Greek Minister of Shipping), M. Lyras, M. Karageorgis, N. Papalios. BELOW LEFT Costa M. Lemos, richest of all Greek shipowners. BELOW RIGHT George Christos Lemos, an elder statesman of Greek shipping, being decorated by Pope Paul VI with the insignia of a Commander of the Order of Pope Gregorius during ecumenical talks in Rome which Lemos attended as a lay member of the Greek Orthodox Church. *photo*: Pontificia Fotografia

Aristotle Onassis on the *Christina* with his beloved El Greco

ABOVE The hostile ex-brothers-in-law Aristotle Onassis and Stavros Niarchos (right), rarely photographed together; left: the late Aly Khan. RIGHT The Livanos sisters, Tina Livanos-Onassis-Blandford-Niarchos and the late Eugenie Niarchos. *photo*: Desmond O'Neill

wills are not published in Greece and Livanos, more than most Greeks, was adept in camouflaging his assets. The Livanos fleet, thirty tankers and thirty dry-cargo ships, altogether over one and a half million tons, was his monument. Unlike other Greek shipping companies largely built on credit, his was almost totally paid up except for six tankers of 68,500 tons each which were on order for him in Japanese shipyards at the time of his death and ten dry-cargo ships a-building in Yugoslavia, total cost £25 million.

The Greek practice is for a quarter of a man's estate to go to his wife and the other three quarters to his children with a heavy bias in favour of the eldest son while daughters cannot expect much apart from their dowry which discharges a father's main obligation to them. Stavros Livanos left his wife Arietta assets worth some £25 million including his homes in Athens, Switzerland and France (an apartment in the Avenue Foch in Paris). Eugenie whose husband was richer than her father and hardly in need of special consideration, was left one of her father's companies, North Pacific Shipping Limited, which controlled four tankers, total tonnage 106,000 tons, but the ships were soon acquired by Niarchos and incorporated into his fleet. Tina whose husband, though wealthy by English standards, was not in the same financial league as his in-laws, was more generously endowed ('Nobody will ever know the exact details,' Lady Blandford said a little puckishly). Like her mother she left her share to be administered by the new head of the Livanos empire.

One of the world's most eligible bachelors, George S. Livanos bravely warded off speculation about his marriage plans, English débutantes and French actresses competed for his favour. Friends thought that his association with King Paul's daughter, Princess Sophie of Greece, was ripening into love, that an engagement was imminent and that George would soon become the first Greek shipowner to marry into the royal family, but the Princess opted for Juan Carlos, the Spanish Pretender and for a possible place by his side on the throne of Spain which may await him after the death of General Franco.

Gossip continued to link George Livanos with many equally attractive, if not quite so exalted, young ladies. The prophets of marriage had to wait another three years and when he made his choice it came as a surprise to them. Early in 1966, he went to a party given by his niece Christina Onassis at her father's Athens villa where he met one of her girl friends, Lita Voivoda, the sixteen year old daughter of the immensely wealthy Greek tobacco manufacturer Statamis Viovoda.

Two months later George asked for Lita's hand. After the obligatory family consultation, her father accepted his proposal. Lita's dowry, big enough even for so rich a groom, was a £10 million share in the Viovoda tobacco business. The young couple exchanged rings and arrangements were made for the wedding to take place at the Greek Orthodox Church in Paris in November of the same year with a civil wedding to follow, as French law demands.

On the eve of the ceremony, George with twenty of his English, Greek and American friends, flew from London for the stag party in a Paris bistro, which lasted until the early hours. He was yet bright and spruce as he went through the involved orthodox ceremony in the candle-lit church. The traditional crown was held over the head of the bride who looked girlish with her shoulder-length hair and visibly over-whelmed by the emotional occasion. Mama Stassa Voivoda wiped a few tears from her eyes. Tina's daughter, Christina Onassis, her step-daughter Henrietta Blandford, and little Maria Niarchos were among the bridesmaids.

The list of people attending the wedding reception was spectacular even for the Paris *Ritz* but some of the wedding presents – a two-engined aircraft, a Rubens and a £10,000 sports car – could not very well be put on display. The youthful bride became mistress of the half dozen homes which are *de rigeur* for a Greek shipping tycoon, and joined the merry-go-round which kept her on the move between the London apartment off Grosvenor Square, the house in Athens, etc., etc.

Apart from Stavros Niarchos casting an occasional sidelong glance at the Livanos ships and hinting that they might be employed more profitably or, perhaps, just differently or even under his admiralship – which was not conducive to good relations with George Livanos – the two fleets sailed along in watchful competition. Under the eyes of the young head of the firm, a small army of clerks administered the Livanos ships in the City of London, in Piraeus and in New York where George invested 25 million dollars in a Fifth Avenue block (corner of 57th Street). The fleet expanded even though brother-in-law Niarchos raced ahead at a speed only equalled by Costa M. Lemos and Aristotle Onassis.

The forty Niarchos companies, his Greek shipyards and some ninety supertankers, embraced assets of close to five hundred million dollars. Business was never better. No more than a tiny cloud on the horizon warned of a stormy passage ahead – not for the ships but for the private lives of the Livanos-Niarchos family. The doom-laden imagination of a Euripides or a Sophocles could not have concocted a tragedy to match the disaster that threatened Stavros and Eugenie Niarchos.

V

DEAL, NO DEAL

AS in the days of the Karamanlis regime when the two "parachutists" in hot competition made their first major investments in Greece – Onassis obtained control of Olympic Airways, the Greek national airline, and Niarchos of Skaramanga – the new rulers of Greece, anxious to attract investment, turned to the Greek shipowners. As of yore, their list of major candidates was automatically headed by Onassis and Niarchos. As with Karamanlis, so with the Colonels – both men showed willing and bid for favourable contracts.

The department in charge of the two-pronged negotiations was the Economics Ministry and the official assigned to juggle terms with Onassis and Niarchos was Rodinos Orlandos, deputy to Nikolaos Makarezos, the Junta's economic overlord. Moving from one to the other, Orlandos kept the talks going. Onassis threw himself into the business with characteristic energy camouflaged by superficial nonchalance.

Onassis deeply involved in a multi-million dollar deal? He was very much in the news but business was thought to be farther from his mind than ever before. Romance was a different matter altogether. The world's newspapers were full of stories about his impending marriage to Jacqueline Kennedy.

But while a large posse of reporters kept their eyes firmly on the prospective bridegroom and hundreds of labourers were getting Skorpios Island ready for the nuptials, Onassis was supervising teams of experts who were busy compiling data about oil refineries, aluminium plants, generating stations and other industrial enterprises which he proposed to finance in Greece.

Feasibility studies, legal opinions, financial calculations grew into big volumes which, as usual, were promptly reduced to the hard core of a few foolscap pages for the man who was making the decisions. He himself, sitting in the 'salon' of *Christina* was on the telephone to the United States, London, Paris, Geneva, talking to industrialists, oil men, aluminium and electricity experts canvassing support for his project. What was at stake was an investment of some 400 million dollars in which, Onassis indicated, the American Reynolds Aluminium Corporation would participate.

The wedding of Ari and Jacki took place on Sunday, October 20, 1968, in the tiny chapel of Skorpios. Hundreds of reporters tried to get on the island which was stoutly defended against invasion. In the scramble some of them were unceremoniously dumped into the sea by guards who circled Ari's private paradise in motorboats. Eventually, if somewhat grudgingly, twelve reporters were admitted, wrote glowing accounts of the ceremony and speculated about the destination of *Christina* which stood by to carry the happy couple off on honeymoon – to the Bahamas, the Caribbean, the Fiji Islands, who knows where.

Onassis was by no means ready to get away from it all, not yet. He and his bride stayed put on Skorpios and, as so often when a Greek tycoon's private life is caught in the limelight, it helped to deflect attention from his business affairs. For Onassis, come to think of it, Skorpios was no more than a commuter's ride away from Athens. His Piaggio aircraft could take him to the capital in little more than an hour. Flying off at the crack of dawn each morning, the bridegroom was at his house in Kifizia in time for breakfast. Most of his days during the first week of his marriage were spent in Athens – evenings, like any loyal groom, he returned to the marital bed in Skorpios.

From conversations with Rodinos Orlandos, Onassis graduated to the office of Prime Minister George Papadopoulos for a decisive meeting. They were discussing the complicated details of the proposed investment programme when the Prime Minister's working schedule, already threatened with disruption, demanded his immediate departure for a public function. This was a crucial moment. It was now or never. They were so near agreement, both men were reluctant to interrupt their talk: 'Come with me in the car,' Papadopoulos suggested.

Riding through the streets of Athens lined with police as every route the Prime Minister travels, they settled outstanding differences and agreed on all major points. Onassis pulled an old envelope from his pocket and scribbled down the four or five main items. Paragraph One of the agreement which covered a period of ten years concerned Onassis' investment in the oil refinery and covered the price and freight rates for crude oil, the basis of the big operation. Other points dealt with the project of an aluminium plant including the supply of cheap electricity. The smoothly flowing signature of 'A. S. Onassis' was appended and the Prime Minister counter-signed with his initials. The deal involved 400 million dollars.

Two days later with public interest in the 'marriage of the century' still unabated, Onassis treated the public to a formal announcement of his latest finance coup. At long last, *Christina* raised anchor and Ari and Jackie departed on their overdue honeymoon.

The Greek Government's simultaneous conversations with Stavros Niarchos were as dramatic. He, too, commuted daily by helicopter from Spetsopoula Island to his offices at Skaramanga. The contract he was negotiating offered him a two-thirds share in the state-owned Aspropyrgos Oil Refinery whose production was to be increased to 4.5 million tons a year, as well as facilities for a major expansion of his 'Hellenic Shipyards'. Another project in the package was a marine engine factory, in view of the rapid growth of shipbuilding in Greece, a most propitious project.

Niarchos would have signed there and then had he not received confidential information about the details of the Onassis deal. He did not like what he heard. The projects and terms offered to him seemed inferior to those Onassis had secured. Already huffed about the attention which his arch enemy's spectacular marriage commanded, Niarchos abruptly broke off his conversations with the Greek Government and departed for Paris and London.

But while the official negotiations hung fire, he, too, was busy on the telephone. He talked to Economics Minister Makarezos, and, as a result, trumped the Onassis amount and offered to stake a total of 500 million dollars producing evidence of substantial support from two major American corporations, Continental Oil Company and Kaiser Aluminium. Makarezos promised Niarchos facilities to build his own oil refinery. When Niarchos continued to sulk, the Greek Vice-President travelled to Paris to persuade him to return to Greece and sign on the dotted line.

Now it was Onassis' turn to be perturbed. It did not take long for the news of the new development to reach him via the *Christina's* crackling radio telephone. Obviously, his own refinery was threatened with serious competition. With Kaiser Aluminium involved, who knows but Niarchos might also challenge him with an aluminium project of his own. This was the end of the honeymoon – the business honeymoon with the Greek Government and the honeymoon cruise with Jackie. Onassis returned to Athens in a vile temper and stormed into the Prime Minister's office demanding that his deal be honoured in spirit as well as in letter. Niarchos should not be allowed to mount a rival operation!

With one stroke, the situation was transformed. It was no longer a matter of Onassis versus Niarchos which was nothing new on the battlefield of tankers and oil. The real contestants were the backers of the two Greeks, Papadopoulos and Makarezos. It was inconceivable that Papadopoulos would go back on his word as an officer and gentleman and equally certain that, in such a contest, the Prime Minister would emerge victorious and the Onassis proposition be upheld. But all was not well with Onassis. The American interests which were propping him up appeared to be not as firmly committed as was thought. Reynolds Aluminium, it turned out, had not given a firm undertaking of support – they were only considering his proposition, no more.

The situation was getting more confused every day, and a period of intense haggling ensured. The two vast projects involving a thousand million dollars were in the balance. Deputy Economics Minister Rodinos Orlandos resigned, a victim – or a scapegoat – of conflicting interests which could not be reconciled. The Greek Government announced that both deals had been scrapped. To gain time, the package was put out to public tender. Several new candidates appeared on the scene and made their bids, British Petroleum, Shell and Mobile among them. Onassis and Niarchos revised their respective propositions and joined in the fray. Not surprisingly, the extraneous bidders were soon eliminated. Before long Onassis and Niarchos were once more the only contenders in the running.

Both soon signed contracts which only marginally differed from the original concept. The Onassis arrangement provided for the Greek Government to put land for his refinery at his disposal – a requisition order for a suitable location at Megara was promptly issued. The contract laid down the price of crude oil and freight rates for the refinery's raw material. The Onassis concept of the new aluminium factory relied on cheap electricity which would considerably reduce the cost of production.

The ink on the agreement was not yet dry when Onassis asked for a revision of several points. He complained that the Greek Government was slow in ratifying the deal. Withal, by the end of 1970, he produced a deposit of seven million dollars as an earnest of his intentions. In spite of the modifications he was seeking, his spokesman said he had every intention of going ahead. 'Omega' Company, brought into being specifically to handle the refinery complex, took a stand at *Posidonia 70'*, the international shipping exhibition in Athens.

Niarchos in the meantime was rapidly going ahead with his part of the bargain. An edge was given to his running battle with Onassis by a clause in his contract which envisaged an increase in the output of the Aspropyrgos refinery (from 4.5 to 6 million tons) if the Onassis refinery should not come into being. He lost no time putting the expansion of his shipyard in hand. Hellenic Shipyards were soon turning out an impressive number of 'SD 14' vessels and were already building bulk carriers of between 30,000 and 35,000 tons. The Mediterranean's largest graving dock (for scraping ship's bottoms), capable of taking vessels of up to 240,00p tons came into being.

While Niarchos was getting on with it, the fog around the Onassis project thickened. The terms of his application for revisions led independent observers to conclude that he was trying to get rid of the whole commitment. Onassis pointed to the new situation in the world's petroleum market created by the rise in oil prices as a result of new agreements between the oil companies and the Persian Gulf countries, problems which could not have been anticipated. Another difficulty arose when the requisition order for the Megara land was contested in the law courts.

The Greek Government still put a brave face on the affair. 'The projects foreseen in the package deal are so important,' said an inspired comment, 'as to render it most unlikely that they will not be carried through.' Such optimism was not justified. As always when confronted with a tricky problem, Onassis went over to the offensive. Far from producing 400 million dollars as the agreement provided, he demanded compensation for estimated losses over the ten year life of the contract.

In the claim he submitted for arbitration, he said that supplying Greece with 64 million tons of crude oil over the next ten years at rates fixed in January 1970, would involve him in a loss of between 810 and 1,100 million dollars. He demanded 160 million dollars compensation for damage as a result of the regime's 'unjustified' delay in ratifying the deal and failure to make the land at Megara available to him within the specified time. The total figure he put on his loss was a gigantic 1,200 million dollars. An alternative submission by his lawyers suggested that if the arbitrators decided that the contract was invalid, their client should be reimbursed to the extent of twenty million dollars for expenses incurred in the preparation of the project.

In his time, Onassis has taken on all comers and challenged America's biggest oil companies ('the seven ugly sisters'), the U.S. Government, the Government of Peru, Prince Rainier of Monaco. He had been tussling with successive Greek Governments over the terms of his airline concessions Traditional Greek shipowners were watching developments in his latest conflict with aloof disdain. The 'parachutist' was at it again. Oh Onassis! Age had not withered his vigour nor marriage mellowed his taste for a fight. There was method in his madness.

He was wriggling out of a deal which no longer looked as attractive as when it was initiated. The shipping situation was changing, American institutions were no longer eager to pour money into European projects, the future of the Greek Government seemed uncertain. In the event the Greek Government and Onassis agreed to cancel the contract. He withdrew his claim for compensation and the Government returned his deposit of seven million dollars performance guarantee.

For once leaving the field to Niarchos, Onassis was already off on a new venture which provided a revealing glimpse of the shipping boom. The vessel involved was a 200,000 ton tanker built for Onassis at a Japanese yard at a cost of 12.5 million dollars. Already tied up for a long-term charter, the tanker was ready for delivery two months earlier than scheduled. Onassis would not dream of leaving her idle for a day, far less for two months. He leased her to Shell for a single trip from the Persian Gulf to Europe – gross revenue around five million dollars. His profit on that single trip covered almost one third of the ship's total cost.

At the same time he realised an ambition which many Greek shipowners cherish. Where a yacht used to be their most desirable status symbol, in the age of diversification they craved for a piece of substantial real estate as a symbol of their wealth. Costa M. Lemos had his Third Avenue block, the Livanos name was carved on one of the Fifth Avenue giants. Now Onassis joined the ranks of the Greek Manhattan landlords. In 1971, he acquired the premises of a department store, Best and Company, next door to the Fifth Avenue office of Olympic Airways which also housed his American shipping company, Victory Carriers. The plan was for the two buildings to be replaced by a skyscraper, projected name: Olympic Towers.

VI

DEATH ON SPETSOPOULA

ST TROPEZ, the quaint little artists' village of yore turned into an international playground. Brigitte Bardot's unadorned charms, albeit hidden behind her garden walls. Scores of less reticent and equally scantily clad French girls on view. Sun-tanned Romeos parading their torsos on the beaches, stalking among the bodies beautiful. Yachts of every shape and size in the harbour, half the people sitting in quayside cafes watching the other half sauntering by. Out at sea, motorboats roaring past swimmers and waterskiers and the less energetic gently propelling themselves forward in water rickshaws with or without engines. Evenings, a dozen discotheques exploding with the beat of exuberant bands.

Charlotte Ford, elder of Henry II's two daughters, was among the many Americans who enjoyed the fun in the season of 1959 – or was it 1960, she cannot exactly remember which. With her sister Anne she made the rounds of cocktails and dinners in intimate restaurants or aboard visiting yachts. Motor rides along the coast and parties at the villas of French magnates were part of the routine. Slight and attractive, sexy with eyes which suggested inner conflict, Charlotte's convent upbringing, as often with a Catholic education, seemed to have kept a tight lid on her perfectly natural emotions and urges which were liable to erupt sooner or later. Her constant escort was young George S. Livanos who was as yet six years away from matrimony.

It was George who suggested that they drive to Cap d'Antibes, near Cannes, where brother-in-law Stavros Niarchos was in residence at the magnificent Chateau de la Croe whose previous occupants were King Leopold of the Belgians, the Duke of Windsor – and Ari Onassis, from under whose feet

Niarchos had literally pulled the chateau's precious rugs. (Ari rented it but had to move out when Stavros bought it.) An added attraction was the Niarchos schooner *Creole* which made cruising an exquisite pleasure for even the most yacht-conditioned millionaire. The Ford girls accepted George's suggestion with alacrity and drove with him to Antibes where they were received by Niarchos.

Friends of the family have intimated that Charlotte, like Jackie Onassis (or Jackie Kennedy, as she then was), liked older men. But her encounter with Niarchos did not bear this out. It was nothing short of a disaster. Years later, brimful with resentment, she gave an account of their first meeting, vague in many respects but very definite on some details. She said Niarchos entertained her and her sister throughout the day, then asked them to stay for dinner and overnight. Charlotte protested that she had nothing to wear but refused to go out and buy a new dress – she was known to be careful with her money – whereupon, according to her, Niarchos called her 'the cheapest thing I ever saw'. She responded no less rudely by telling him that he was 'a bloody bore' and 'a dirty old man'. He was, in fact, thirty-two years older than she and, incidentally, eight years older than her father.

And that, for the time being, was that. Charlotte Ford and Stavros Niarchos went their own ways which only occasionally crossed at parties in Paris, London or New York, but they hardly talked. Romance was in Charlotte's bad books at the moment. She and her sister Anne took it badly when their father and mother parted after twenty-three years of marriage. The girls blamed the break-up on their new stepmother, Cristina Austin, Italian-born ex-wife of a British naval officer, and for a long time refused to talk to the second Mrs Henry Ford II.

They were in St Moritz in January 1965, five years after the unhappy outing to Cap d'Antibes. George Livanos was still around and pleaded with Charlotte to put the memory of that day behind her. Not in his wildest dreams could he foresee that he was, however, obliquely, paving the ground for his own sister's tragedy. The Niarchos chalet was one of the marvels of Europe's premier winter-sports resort, and George thought Charlotte and Anne would enjoy joining his brother-in-law there for dinner one evening. The sisters were persuaded to accept Stavros Niarchos' invitation but when they arrived for what they expected to be a small dinner and perhaps a film show they discovered that there were another dozen guests, among them – to their embarrassment – their father and his new wife.

It turned out to be a fortuitous encounter which enabled Charlotte to get to know her step-mother better. She was captivated by Cristina's charm and found her to be very amusing: 'She makes you roll on the floor laughing,' she said. It was the beginning of a close friendship – two friendships. Throughout the evening, Niarchos could hardly take his eyes off Charlotte. The other guests noticed, Cristina noticed. Charlotte noticed. What Eugenie Niarchos thought has not been recorded. The following day Charlotte and Stavros went skiing together. Stavros took her out to dinner – in the next two weeks they skiied and dined together a lot.

That summer, Niarchos was cruising in *Creole* in the Mediterranean while Charlotte and Anne were with their father in Sir Bernard and Lady Docker's yacht *Shemara* which was almost as opulently equipped as Onassis' *Christina*. *Creole* constantly zigzagged across the path of *Shemara* while messages passed back and forth. Whenever *Shemara* put into port along the French and Italian Riviera *Creole* followed. Niarchos and the Fords got together for joint dinners ashore or aboard one of the yachts. Niarchos drank less than usual and was his most charming self whenever he was in Charlotte's company. Still, nobody guessed the full story.

At worst, Henry Ford suspected his daughter had a crush on the middle-aged Greek shipowner. It was much more than a crush. Not many weeks passed before Charlotte told her father that she and Stavros planned to get married: 'He nearly had a heart attack,' she recalled. The little matter of

78

Stavros' marriage to Eugenie was dealt with by a quickie divorce. He gave Charlotte an engagement ring of some forty carats which cost more than half a million dollars and was invariably referred to by the Ford family as 'the skating rink'. The couple were married at Juarez, Mexico, before the year was out, went on honeymoon to Nassau in Henry Ford's private jet. A chartered Boeing 707 took them to Zurich whence they drove to St Moritz.

For three months they stayed together. 'The only married life I knew,' Charlotte said. It ended when she flew to New York where she moved into the Niarchos triplex to await the arrival of her baby. Her husband came on a short visit when she gave birth to a baby girl who was christened Elena. The scene quickly shifts to Antibes and the Chateau de la Croe where the couple were due to be reunited. Charlotte was there waiting for Niarchos but he never turned up. Instead he sent a message that he was going on safari with his son Spiros who was not taking his parents' separation well. Next, one of his friends went to see Charlotte and told her that Stavros wanted a divorce. By this time he was back from Africa and back with – Eugenie. Charlotte's marriage, or whatever it was, was as good as over. Fourteen months after the Juarez wedding there was a divorce in Juarez.

So far, my account has largely followed Charlotte's own version of her meeting with Niarchos, their engagement and marriage. Long after it was all over she said she was sure that she was the only woman Nicharos ever really loved. But there was another version of this bizarre interlude which originated from Greek shipowners' circles. Niarchos' compatriots were incensed at the treatment which one of the 'parachutists' had meted out to the daughter of the fondly remembered and revered Stavros Livanos. They called it "public humiliation" and worse. What had happened, they said, was that Charlotte Ford did, in fact, have a crush on Niarchos with consequences not uncommon even in the best circles and that Henry Ford, not surprisingly, had been livid. He was said to have bluntly ordered Niarchos to marry his daughter – or else!

The wrath of one of America's richest and most influential men – still according to the Greek interpretation – was something not even Niarchos could contemplate lightly. Besides, while marriage may not have been his original intention, he liked Charlotte well enough. Rather than make an implacable enemy of Ford, he is said to have taken the marriage vows for a fourth time – with a mental reservation which soon became apparent. Though it does not forbid divorce and re-marriage, the Greek Orthodox Church allows one man three marriages but no more. Thus, even before Charlotte's marriage was formally dissolved, it did not exist in the eyes of the Church to which Niarchos belonged and, perhaps, not in his own eyes either. When questions were raised about his reunion with Eugenie, he instructed a spokesman to say that there was no need for a re-marriage because, church-wise, the marriage to Charlotte, his fourth marriage, was in any case null and void.

Although Charlotte summed up her experiences with a bitter sigh – 'I know now what it means to be married to a Greek' – her parting from Stavros turned out to be as unconventional as his temporary separation from Eugenie. Before and after the Juarez divorce, Charlotte and her ex-non-husband met frequently 'to discuss the future of little Elena'. Charlotte waived alimony for herself but asked Stavros to provide for their daughter. The settlement he suggested was generous beyond anything she had contemplated. They continued to see each other and Niarchos followed his daughter's progress with a fond father's interest.

For Eugenie, the reunion with her husband was soured by his constant preoccupation with Charlotte, a burden difficult to bear. A sensitive, vulnerable woman not conditioned to such complications, she was seen less and less in public and spent as much time as possible in the impregnable seclusion of Spetsopoula Island. As she withdrew into herself, Stavros Niarchos increasingly relied on Tina for help and advice about her sister's difficulties. But Spetsopoula's defences against uninvited guests could not prevent the intrusion of profound private grief which became dramatically apparent in the summer of 1970.

As if to deepen the gloom on Spetsopoula, it was raining hard all Sunday, May 3, 1970, most unlike the celebrated springtime in the Aegean and not the kind of weather to lift the deep depression from Eugenie Niarchos. Her husband was not in a happy frame of mind either. Throughout the afternoon, in the big drawing room of their villa, the couple argued and shouted at each other. Eugenie was in tears.

Since they were alone, stories about the deeper cause of their quarrel are bound to be speculation and largely informed by hindsight. One of them suggested that Eugene resented Stavros' habit of discussing their marital affairs with Tina, however naturally a husband might turn to his wife's sister for help and advice. Then there was the aggravating argument about little Elena.

They were quarrelling about Elena. Charlotte's daughter was four and Stavros apparently wanted her to spend a few weeks with him on the island. Genie said No! Though she felt no malice towards the child she would no longer suffer in silence. As she had said on previous occasions, Elena's presence would be a constant reminder of her husband's excursion into another woman's arms. It was more than she could stand. It was intolerable.

There is no doubt that the row flared up and subsided and flared up again. There were recriminations and accusations, reconciliation and new outbreaks. It would seem that Stavros remained adamant about Elena's visit. At nine p.m. he picked up the telephone and called his New York apartment at Sutton Place where Charlotte and the child were staying. Listening with mounting despair, Eugenie heard him asking Charlotte to make arrangement for the child to be sent to Greece as soon as possible.

For Genie it was utter defeat. Much of what happened next emerged from the police investigation which followed. She went upstairs to her bedroom to find release from her misery in sleep but anger and unhappiness kept her awake. She reached for her bottle of Seconal and swallowed two tablets, her usual dose. Still sleep would not come. After tossing and turning for a while she got up and went downstairs. With only a bottle of whisky to keep him company, Stavros' temper had not improved. The quarrel started all over again until Eugenie again escaped to her bedroom. Again she reached for the Seconal bottle – and swallowed the lot, some forty tablets.

Stavros also went up to his bedroom but could not sleep either. It was ten-thirty p.m. Genie had been so desperate, he decided to talk to her once more. Entering her bedroom he saw her lying in bed in her flimsy nightdress. She looked pale. No sign of breathing. The empty bottle of Seconal on the floor told its own story. Had she taken too many? Was it possible that, befuddled by the earlier dose, she had misjudged the amount? Or had she deliberately swallowed all the tablets to finish it all?

For a man at the end of an unnerving day – and a bottle of whisky – it was a terrifying discovery. Stavros tried to rouse his wife but she did not respond. This was no ordinary sleep. It would take more than a gentle pat to awaken her from the stupor. He shook her, gripping her hard by the shoulders, his strong arms frantically clutching her slender body. Wake up, wake up! He slapped her mouth and pushed his finger deep towards her larynx to make her retch. With growing apprehensions, he pressed his hand against her abdomen to make her body give up the poison, lifted her and tried to stand her on her head. Now near panic he slapped her hard, shook her again and again, tilted her – anything to bring her back to consciousness. Get rid of the poison, get rid of the poison! Somehow, anyhow! Nothing else mattered. It was of no avail.

There are situations when even the most sophisticated man no longer fully knows what he is doing. In this emotion-charged hour when Genie did not respond to shock treatment, a feeling of helplessness, totally out of character with a man accustomed to wield great power, was bound to produce a violent reaction. But this was one problem toughness could not solve.

Stavros Niarchos needed help. His first thought was to summon Angelo Markini, his valet and confidant, until he remembered that this was his day off. Still hoping against hope that Eugenie could be roused from her unconsciousness and the whole tragic incident resolved and forgotten, he would not call the maid on whose discretion he could not be sure.

Hope was fading. What was needed, urgently, desperately needed, was a doctor. No point fetching the ageing local man from neighbouring Spetsai Island, some ten minutes motor-boat ride away. How could he leave Genie alone? Instead he telephoned his sister, Mary Dracopoulos, in Athens and asked her to get in touch with Dr Panayotis Arnaoutis, the Skaramanga Works doctor, and send him to the island. Within minutes, Dr Arnaoutis was alerted. He rushed to Evangelismos Hospital to pick up a stomach pump and other instruments before boarding the Niarchos helicopter which took him to Spetsopoulos.

It was half an hour past midnight when the doctor landed and went to the villa. By this time Eugenie Niarchos was beyond help. Dr Arnaoutis told Niarchos that his wife was dead: 'You will have to inform the police'. Niarchos was too distraught to speak to a stranger. He telephoned Cristos Michaelopoulos, his financial director and right-hand man and said: 'We have had a terrible accident. Please tell the police'.

When told by Michaelopoulos what had happened on Spetsopoula, Spetsai Police Chief Kotronis raced across by motorboat. It was three a.m. when he arrived at the Niarchos villa. He promptly decided that this was a matter for medical experts and telephoned the mainland to summon two forensic scientists, Dr Kapsaskis and Dr Georgios Agioutantis, Professor of Forensic Medicine at the University of Athens.

Kapsaskis was no stranger to difficult and controversial medical situations – it was he who conducted a post-mortem on Lambrakis, the left-wing member of parliament who was murdered in Salonika in 1963, and certified 'death as a result of a motorbike accident'. (The killing of Lambrakis by political opponents is the subject of the famous film *X* which anti-Junta Greeks interpret as an indictment of the military regime although it did not exist at the time.)

Dr Kapsaskis refused to go to Spetsopoula and explained that a laboratory examination was essential. Accompanied by Kotronis and Arnoutis the body was flown to Athens at the same time as Constantine Fafoutis, the Piraeus Public Prosecutor, flew to Spetsopoula to interview Niarchos and the servants and to study the situation on the spot. On his return to Piraeus Fafoutis formally announced that 'Pending an investigation to determine whether a culpable act has been committed, the Office of the Public Prosecutor of Piraeus has requested Mr Stavros Niarchos not to leave the country'. Niarchos was set bail in the sum of 500,000 Drachmae (£6,000).

Four days later, on May 12, Doctors Kapsaskis and Agioutantis, having conducted a post-mortem examination, produced a Report (No. 5171/1970) which listed fourteen injuries on the body of Eugenie Niarchos. They included a bruise on the left eye and swelling on the left temple; an eliptic haemorrhage on the right side of the neck, apparently the result of pressure by a finger; three parallel smaller bruises in the shape of fingerprints on the left side of the neck above the collarbone; injuries to the skin below and the fibres of the muscle; a haemorrhage to the left of the larynx; a two inch bruise on the abdomen with internal bleeding and bleeding behind the diaphragm in the region of the fourth and fifth vertebra; bruises on the left arm; bruises on the left ankle and the left shin; finally a bruise on the ring finger and a tear on the little finger of the left hand. The Report concluded that the injuries were due to 'old-fashioned attempts at resuscitation'. Death, according to the toxicological analysis, was caused by an overdose of sleeping tablets.

Public Prosecutor Fafoutis brushed these findings aside. The injuries he declared unequivocally, were the result of blows from fists and of kicks and 'a perfect strangling mechanism'. Stavros Niarchos would be indicted for doing 'wilful bodily harm resulting in death'. Confronted with these contradictory assessments, the investigating magistrate of Piraeus instructed his own forensic experts. Doctors Anastasios Sylantavos and Konstantinos Boukis to undertake a new examination. Their report, issued the following month, suggested that 'the collapse and death of Eugenie Niarchos' was due to the injuries diagnosed by Doctors Kapsaskis and Agioutantis, and that the quantity of Seconal (two milligrams barbiturate in a hundred cubic centimetres of blood) taken by the deceased could not have produced a fatal effect which would have required three milligrams of barbiturates in the same volume of blood.

Since this new view of the cause of death confused the issue still further, the investigating magistrate set up a tribunal of experts composed of Doctors Kapsaskis, Agioutantis, Sylantavos and Boukis plus two Athens university professors, Konstantinos Tountas (surgeon) and Dionysios Varonos (experimental pharmacologist). Niarchos was permitted to nominate two further experts – Professors Konstantinos Alevizatos (surgeon) and Konstantinos Moiras (biological chemist) – who were co-opted. The eight-man tribunal studied the evidence and handed down their conclusion: 'The injuries found on the body were slight, and Eugenie Niarchos was already in a comatose condition when they occurred. They did not contribute to the fatality which was partly due to the effects of Seconal and partly to the action intended to revive the deceased'.

It had taken three medical examinations and two harassing months under the shadow of the Public Prosecutor's nightmarish insinuations to lift the burden of an absurd suspicion from the hapless Niarchos who was still confined to Spetsopoula Island. To demonstrate its belief in his innocence, the Greek Government chose the ceremonial inauguration of a new dry dock at the Hellenic Shipyard at Skaramanga. With young Philip Niarchos representing his father, the Junta's Number Three, Nikolaos Makarezos, Minister for Economic Coordination, named the dry dock *Eugenie Niarchos*. Unveiling a plaque with her name, he said: 'We are confident that the inspirator and creator of this shipyard will face the blows of fate with the same courage which enabled the ancient Greeks to triumph over the power of death'. Eugenie's remains were taken from Piraeus to Spetsopoula where they were buried. The ban on Niarchos leaving the country was lifted and he sailed away in *Creole* to cruise in the Mediterranean. The nightmare was over. Or was it?

Fafoutis still had a few arrows to his bow. The Niarchos case, it seemed had unleashed a power struggle between pro-Junta judges and their opponents who were anxious to demonstrate their independence from political pressures. The implication was that the Junta wanted to get Niarchos off the hook while anti-Junta judges were determined that he should be prosecuted. Be that as it may, Fafoutis announced grandiloquently that he was going to do his duty. On August 22, he produced a forty-four page document (Protocol 698/22.8.1970) in which the whole case was summed up.

Setting out the sequence of events as he saw them, Fafoutis' first point was that the Spetsai police chief Kotronis was looking for sleeping tablets in Eugenie's bedroom but was told by Dr Arnaoutis that neither sleeping tablets nor an empty phial had been found. Fafoutis next contested the toxicological analysis on the grounds that the organs of the deceased (brain, kidneys, intestines) had been preserved in a formalin solution for two months before being submitted for examination. This was against the procedure as laid down in K. Iliakis' *Forensic Medicine* (Volume A, Pg. 18) which neither permitted delay nor the addition of preservatives.

'If death had occurred as a result of barbiturates' Fafoutis stated, 'the body would have taken on a pink or light red colour (K. Iliakis *Ibid.*, Volume A, Pg. 40) which was not the case. Hence the cause of death must be found elsewhere.' That the injuries were caused by attempts to rouse the unconscious woman was, according to him, 'outside the realm of likelihood'. As represented by Stavros Niarchos himself, Fafoutis added, the facts exclude suicide by Seconal and this was borne out by the autopsy. It was a case of maltreatment with a fatal outcome.

After going in to the matter of Niarchos' telephone conversation with Charlotte Ford, the Public Prosecutor continued: "Niarchos claims to have gone to bed after the telephone conversation and to have turned out the light but decided – at about ten twenty-five p.m. – to explain the invitation to Ford to his wife, to have gone to her bedroom and found her unconscious on the bed. Assuming that she had taken sleeping tablets, he claims to have, for this reason, slapped her and shaken her, etc., etc.

'These claims,' Fafoutis went on, 'provoke several questions:

'1. Why, such a long time after the telephone conversation, did he decide to give his wife further explanations? 2. Why, when he entered her bedroom and found her asleep, did he regard this as suspicious since he himself also went to sleep after the telephone conversation? Was it not possible that his wife had found sleep more quickly than he, either quite naturally or with the help of her usual dose of sleeping pills which, according to him, he knew she was in the habit of taking? 3. If she was asleep, why did he rouse her considering that the subject of Ford was no longer so tragic and urgent as to warrant waking her up?"

At the same time Fafoutis listed other reactions by Stavros Niarchos which he deemed suspicious: 'Why did he telephone his valet Angelos Markini who was absent at the time and not a member of the staff in the villa, for instance the very trustworthy maid? (Fafoutis said she was trustworthy: Niarchos was not so sure.) Why should he have called the valet to help the lady of the house who, according to husband and valet, was wearing only a nightgown and not even pants?

"Why not her own maid? Why was no other member of the staff summoned to help? Finally, why, when Niarchos, as he said, noticed that this was a matter of poisoning by barbiturates, did he not summon the Spetsai doctor who could have arrived within minutes and administered first aid independently of Dr Arnaoutis who had to come from Athens and arrived two hours later?" Fafoutis' conclusion was that Niarchos, in

87

the course of a quarrel in Eugenie's bedroom at around ten p.m., 'beat her brutally and thus caused the injuries diagnosed by the forensic experts'. Accordingly, either she or someone else could have administered the sleeping tablets.

The Public Prosecutor demanded the institution of proceedings under Paragraphs 52 and 311 of the Greek Penal Code (which provides for sentence of between five and twenty years imprisonment) 'against Stavros Niarchos, son of Spiros, born in Piraeus, resident in St Moritz, Switzerland, temporarily at Spetsopoula, aged sixty, shipowner of Greek nationality and of Greek Orthodox faith'.

The indictment accused Niarchos of setting out deliberately in the night of May 3 to May 4 to commit a crime, namely inflicting bodily harm which resulted in the death of his spouse, Eugenie Niarchos, aged forty-two. Since the deed had the character of a crime, he demanded the arrest of the accused under Articles 282 and 315 and the institution of proceedings.

The Niarchos side answered with counter blasts firing from many guns. Stavros' nephew, Konstantinos Dracopoulos, son of his sister Mary and manager of Hellenic Shipyards, dismissed the Public Prosecutor's accusations out of hand: 'He can say what he likes – we have the opinion of the medical experts!' Niarchos' legal advisers in several countries went into action against what looked more like a deliberate campaign of persecution than a prosecution. In Paris Maître Réné de Chambrun fulminated: 'I cannot understand what has prompted Prosecutor Fafoutis to make these new and obviously baseless accusations. My client is not in jeopardy. No court would find him guilty.'

The assessment was quite correct. After studying the Fafoutis document and all available evidence, three judges of the Piraeus High Court, Parmenion Zifras, Georgios Trichas and Kyriakos Varvaresos rejected the indictment and declared that the evidence showed convincingly that Eugene Niarchos had committed suicide in the night of May 3 and 4 (Protocol No. 775/1970).

The period in which this decision could have been contested

by the Public Prosecutor ended on Saturday, October 3. He raised no official objections. The case against Stavros Niarchos was closed. Anti-Niarchos elements tried to keep the pot boiling maintaining that political pressure prevented Fafoutis from taking the matter further. George S. Livanos and Lady Blandford met to decide what steps to take – the implication was that a private prosecution was being considered which, in the light of future developments, was quite ridiculous. Onassis was said to have pressed for such a course but there is no evidence, no evidence at all, that he intervened in any way.

The family, particularly Lady Blandford, was concerned with the well-being of the two younger Niarchos children who sorely missed their mother. 'Auntie Tina' was their closest relative, and it was natural for her to look after them. To get them away from the scene of tragedy she took them to England where they stayed with her at the Blandford country house. It was she who made arrangements for them to enter a school in Paris, the same at which her own children received their early education.

With people of such international notoriety involved in a human drama, it was not surprising that rumour ran riot. But there was no evidence to support whispers that relations between Stavros Niarchos and George Livanos were strained or that Niarchos was pressing his late wife's brother to give up some of his ships to him. Arietta Livanos firmly ranged herself by the side of her bereaved son-in-law, and Tina's association with her late sister's husband was never disturbed – on the contrary.

Suggestions that Niarchos was a broken man, that he was ready to give up control of his interests to his son and anxious to retire to Spetsopoula to worship at the grave of his wife, were wide of the mark. Not many months passed before he was back in circulation, was seen in St Moritz in the company of Yul Brynner's beautiful ex-wife and other attractive women although, again, the gossips were wrong to attach any special significance to his social activities.

There was more substance in the talk about his growing

affection for his sister-in-law and, when it became known a little later that Tina Blandford was seeking a divorce from the marquess, it seemed more than possible that there was more to her friendship with Niarchos than either of them would admit. Nor was it surprising that the tragedy had thrown together two people who were already close and had both experienced great suffering. Tina took a house in Villefranche in the South of France overlooking the sea, where the Niarchos schooner *Creole* was moored within view. Her sister's children were with her, and there was a great deal of to-ing and fro-ing between villa and yacht. Persistent reports spoke of an impending marriage but Niarchos, apparently angrily, denied that he intended to marry again.

Cynics put little store by the denial. They remembered that Niarchos always coveted what Onassis possessed – a Livanos daughter for a wife, tankers as big as his rival's, the house (Chateau la Croe) where Onassis lived, a stake in the Greek economy and now, apparently – the woman who used to be Mrs Aristotle Onassis.

VII

DIVORCE AND MARRIAGE

SUCH was the curiosity generated by the alchemy of Ari Onassis' millions and Jackie Kennedy's doom-laden glamour that newspapers and magazines the world over could deny their readers information and gossip about the couple only at their peril: 'The French are probably right,' Onassis told me with a sigh quoting one of his favourite proverbs: *"Pour être heureux il faut vivre en cachette!"* Had their happiness depended on obscurity, the outlook for him and Jackie would have been grim.

A warm-hearted woman carrying the burden of awesome memories with remarkable dignity, Jackie became the target of a barrage of disclosures from former employees who distorted her words and misinterpreted her sentiments to adjust them to the persistent demand for keyhole news about her. What the secretary saw and the steward heard appeared between hard covers and turned up in the bestseller charts. Americans who once adored her as a cultured First Lady of charm and beauty, and commiserated with her as a tragic widow, seemed to feel jilted and resentful when she remarried – their sweetheart deserting them for 'that Greek'!

In an orgy of debunking which replaced the heroine worship, the American goddess of yore was suddenly presented as mean, avaricious, pedantic, egomaniac and, altogether, insufferable. Curiosity persisted unabated and she was constantly besieged by reporters and photographers assigned to satisfy it. The world became her prison – to avoid attention, her Atlantic passages were booked in the name of 'Mrs Simpson'; Colin Simpson, an Onassis associate in London, lending his name as a convenient pseudonym.

If the world was her prison, New York condemned her to

solidarity confinement. She could not leave her apartment in Fifth Avenue (to which her husband transferred from his permanent suite at the *Pierre Hotel*) without bumping into the press. It was the price she paid for maintaining her American associations, for insisting on bringing up her and the late President Kennedy's children as Americans in American schools. When she did venture out, she varied her routine, dressed inconspicuously – anything to protect her privacy. It was of no avail. Occasionally her temper snapped – the day she and Ari went to see the sexy film *I am Curious, Yellow*, there was a rowdy confrontation with a photographer who tracked her down to the cinema. Ari slipped away so as not to escalate the commotion.

Another photographer, Ronald Galella who specialised in candid Jackie Onassis photographs followed her to Central Park when she went cycling with her daughter Caroline. Cameras were smashed, her private guard tried to protect her and the police were called in. The chase ended in court when Galella sued his victim alleging false arrest, malicious prosecution and interference with his livelihood claiming 1.5 million dollars damages. In a counter action Jackie accused Galella of harassment and demanded a similar amount in compensation.

In court she heard herself described as 'the personification of an American dream'. For her it was a nightmare. Giving evidence on her own behalf she said: 'I live in dread fear that the moment I step on the sidewalk that man will assault me – I dare not take my son John to the doctor . . . I promised my daughter to take her shopping but under the circumstances I would not dare to go out.' She described an occasion when Galella rushed down the aisle of a Broadway theatre to take flashlight pictures of her: 'A general uproar ensued and I was humiliated,' Jackie declared. There was another scene when the photographer turned up at the restaurant she visited after the show.

The court's decision was eventually handed down in July 1972. Judge Irving Cooper dismissed Galella's claim for damages and ordered him in future not to approach within fifty yards of Jackie Onassis or within one hundred yards of her home. Galello was also ordered to stay at least seventy-five yards from her children and one hundred yards from their school, and furthermore enjoined from using any pictures he may have taken of Jackie for advertising or trade purposes. Lest the verdict be regarded as an infringement of the freedom of the Press, Judge Cooper suggested that 'Galella was more a self-aggrandizing businessman than an authentic journalist". Jackie had won a glorious victory.

Away from the United States, the pressure on her was not so severe. In Britain Ari and Jackie even came out into the open of their own free will. To support a bid for a majority shareholding in the Northern Ireland Harland and Wolff shipyard, they staged a well managed publicity operation in the course of which they entertained the yard's workers at a party. Organised by Nigel Neilson, Ari's skilful friend and public relations expert, this was the kind of publicity they did not mind. Alas, the Onassis bid for Harland and Wolff was blocked by the British Government which did not want the important industrial complex to come under foreign control.

The couple's visits to Jackie's sister Lee Radziwill at her London town house and in the country attracted only discreet attention from the press with the result that Jackie mellowed sufficiently on one occasion to cross the road outside *Claridge's* Hotel to greet a photographer whose face looked familiar. Yet, the truce was short-lived. When she left London, it was reported that she and Ari had a violent quarrel in the V.I.P. lounge at Heath Row Airport: 'Nonsense!' Ari said and pleaded with the press to leave them alone.

Not a hope. Intermittent reports insisted that Jackie was spending all her husband's money – not easy with a man worth 400 million dollars at a conservative estimate and hard to reconcile with her alleged parsimony; that she was dickering with another man – this based on an old photograph showing her in animated conversation with the architect who built

Ari's house on Skorpios; or that she and Ari were on the verge of divorce, a recurrent rumour. They no longer bothered to deny these reports. Only when Christian Kafarakis, the *Christina's* ex-steward, claimed knowledge of their marriage contract supposed to contain one hundred and seventy clauses about the disposition of the Onassis property, largely in the direction of Jackie, did Ari perk up: 'Not a bit of truth in it!' he said.

But it was quite true that Onassis' lawyers were busy negotiating changes in an important sector of his interests. They were working on a reconstruction of the American Onassis Trust whose value was estimated to have reached around 200 million dollars, three-quarters originally assigned to the American-born Onassis children and twenty-five per cent, the maximum allowed to a foreigner under the maritime laws, in Onassis' own name. The children's share, you may remember, was due to come under their direct control on Christina Onassis' twenty-first birthday, December 11, 1971.

Since, under the maritime laws, it was immaterial on whom the major share would devolve as long as control remained in American hands, it was always open to Onassis to vary the terms of the Trust. As the husband of an American wife, it was not unreasonable to expect that he would want to include her among the beneficiaries, and this was the principal change he asked his lawyers to transact. At the same time, he decided to change the date – Christina's twenty-first birthday – on which the Trust was intended to relinquish control to the beneficiaries.

Assuming that the new construction did not violate the letter and spirit of the maritime laws, there could be no possible objection to the introduction of Jackie's name. But the trustees would want a good reason for his decision to extend the validity of the Trust beyond the original date. It was a delicate matter but a matter between Onassis and the trustees alone which did not need to be ventilated in public. The trustees were told that Onassis was wrestling with a family problem, that he was acting in the best interest of his children . . .

94

Growing up as the children of one of the world's richest men, constantly on the move from Paris apartment to yacht, from yacht to chateau, from Riviera to Athens, or private island, from Europe to the United States, young Alexander and his sister could not escape the peculiar pressures of their jet-set background. The parting of their parents in the late fifties broke the only permanent fixture in their peripatetic existence but – much to the credit of Ari and Tina – links with both parents remained intact. Alexander, as may be expected, came perhaps a little closer to his father, Christina to her mother. Neither took kindly to Ari's much-publicised friendship with Maria Callas whom they blamed for the break-up of their parents' marriage. Still, Onassis kept his life skilfully in compartments and no outward difficulty arose.

Alexander was maturing fast, accompanied his father on trips to London, Paris and the United States, frequently sitting in on business conferences which Onassis conducts in informal, convivial drawing-room settings. More interested in aeroplanes than in tankers, the young man learned to fly and earned his pilot's licence. Onassis père put him in charge of the Olympic Airways Greek island helicopter service which profited from Alexander's energy and flair for organisation.

The only fly, or butterfly, in the ointment was the very beautiful Fiona Thyssen, ex-wife of an immensely wealthy German-Swiss industrialist and previously, as Fiona Campbell-Walter, a well-known British model girl. Fifteen years older than Alexander she became – in the language of the gossip columns from which he temporarily displaced the older Onassis generation – his 'inseparable companion'. Visiting Fiona, Alexander, with a dash of his father's flamboyance, piloted his helicopter between the Greek mainland and the island where she spent a holiday. He joined Fiona in St. Moritz where she lived with her children, and together they turned up in Paris and London.

A man of the world, Ari Onassis watched them from afar and not without some apprehension. While reports of a rift between father and son over Fiona were exaggerated, it was no secret that the prospect of Alexander marrying an older woman did not commend itself to Onassis. When tackled about the problem he shrugged off the association as a young man's passing fancy but if he hoped it would soon end, he was kept waiting for a long time.

The affair was running its natural course when speculation seized on Christina's fast approaching twenty-first birthday. In ignorance of the legal moves around the Trust, friends of the family and the Greek shipping fraternity expected Alexander to come into his 75 million dollar share of the Trust and assumed that, once financially independent, he would marry Fiona with or without his father's consent. They were wrong on both counts.

He was not getting the Trust property and Fiona admitted sadly that there was little likelihood that she and Alexander would ever marry. She was acutely aware of Onassis' opposition because of the difference in their ages: 'And it is quite right,' she added sensibly. Besides, she and Alexander did not have all that much in common – he liked cities, she was an out-door person. Neither did she enjoy his kind of itinerant life, flying here, there, everywhere. No, Ari Onassis had little to worry on that score.

Ari's worry was no longer Alexander but Christina. Christina seemed upset when her father married Jackie Kennedy – it was not tears of joy she shed at the wedding on Skorpios – but there was no deep-seated resentment against her handsome new step-mother. While she had totally rejected Maria Callas, she came to accept Jackie as a friend and admired her *savoir faire*, erudition and, as important, clothes sense. What appealed to her most was Jackie's typically American independence in stark contrast with Greek tradition which allows women far less freedom and, for instance, expects a subservient daughter to await her father's choice of a groom.

Ari counted himself lucky that Christina's first regular boy-friend happened to be the kind of young man any Greek shipowner would be proud to have as his son-in-law. When

Philip Niarchos (far left), deputising for his father Stavros Niarchos (at that time subject to investigation into his wife's death on Spetsopoula) at the opening of an extension to the Skaramanga Shipyard near Athens, in the summer of 1970

A watercolour of the 1880 Greek barque *Anastasia* painted by Manuel Kulukundis during his conversation with the author

ΑΝΑSTAΣΙΑ
a Greek Barque 1 1880

M. Kulukundis
1970

Bluey Mavroleon, now General Manager of London and Overseas Freighters, as a young Guards officer during the last war

Basil Mavroleon
photo: Baron

Christina met young Peter Goulandris in the Bahamas and formed a close friendship with him, it looked as if the Onassis name would once more be linked with that of an outstanding Greek shipping family (whom we shall get to know better a few chapters further on). The romance between Christina and Peter seemed to flourish although the attractive girl with her father's profile and her mother's vivacity led a life of her own and set herself up in an apartment in London's Mayfair in the same block as uncle George Livanos' *pied à terre*. Tina frequently used the apartment when Christina, as becomes the daughter of the biggest jet-setter of them all, flitted from continent to continent.

Their friends were surprised when she and Peter Goulandris drifted apart and even more so when, somewhere along the line and out of her father's reach, she turned up in Los Angeles and became involved in a new romance which puzzled all who knew her. The new man in her life was one Joseph Bolker, recently divorced Hollywood real estate man, twenty-seven years older than she and father of four teenage children. They were a disparate couple – the rich society girl herself only just out of her teens and this grey-haired Lothario who let it be known that he loved serious music and was interested in social work. He was said to be prosperous, 'a millionaire', though by Onassis standards one million does not amount to much. The affair was obviously serious and looked like repeating the pattern of love and marriage set by grandfather Livanos and followed by her father who were both over twenty years older than their wives – in Onassis' second marriage the age difference was as great.

On July 26, 1971, just five months away from her twenty-first birthday, Christina flew from London to Las Vegas where she was met by her ageing *amant du cœur*. That day they were secretly married in a three-minute civil ceremony performed by District Judge Carl Christensen but the secret was short-lived and was soon on the wire services. The news came as a great shock to Aristotle Onassis whose consent had neither been sought nor given. It raised big financial issues – the question of a dowry which is a sacred Greek institution and the structure of the Trust.

Greeks who keep a close eye on the interplay of money and marriage, enviously contemplated the day when Joseph Bolker through his young wife and via the Californian laws on marital community property might become entitled to a share in Onassis' American shipping fortune, a thought not toally absent from Onassis' own mind. Indeed, it was with some such disastrous possibility in view that he had initiated the drastic Trust changes.

Since every international shipping operation affects the market, it was not only from a sense of curiosity that Greek shipowners, as yet ignorant of the Trust negotiations, examined the Californian laws to divine the future of the Onassis tankers. They concluded that, whether the marriage lasted or not, Joseph Bolker might well end up with half of his bride's Trust property or an estimated 35 million dollars worth of tankers. Indeed, this would have been the position if Christina came into the property on her twenty-first birthday – and after her marriage. On the other hand, if it could be shown that the property became technically hers when the Trust was created – that is long before her marriage – it could not be classified as community property.

The argument was purely academic. Even while it went on the lawyers put the finishing touches on arrangements to move the Trust companies and their ships beyond Christina and Joseph Bolker's reach. The groom, it should be said, emphatically repudiated any suggestion that the wealth of Onassis was a factor in his association with Christina: 'We married because we are in love,' he said.

For Ari Onassis it was not only a matter of preventing his tankers from coming under the control of an outsider in whose hands – in an industry which depends on experience, reputation and the personal touch – even such a proud fleet could quickly deteriorate. Important as these considerations were, the implications of his daughter's marital extravaganza on their relationship were even more painful. She had not confided in him, far less consulted him or sought his approval. For the first time there was a serious break between him and a child he fondly loved and who seemed to be slipping away from him into the arms of a man of whom he knew nothing. He left Christina in no doubt about his feelings. Her and her husband's bags were already packed for a flight to Greece, when a curt message told her that Mr Bolker would not be welcome on Skorpios. It was a terrible blow to Christina.

Onassis was hurt and in a fighting mood but no man is more adept at retrieving an awkward situation than he. If it should turn out that Christina had married on a sudden impulse, if she could be made to see the error of her ways, all was not lost, his daughter was not lost and the marriage could be as quickly dissolved as it was contracted. He talked to Christina over the transatlantic telephone, sent Alexander to see her, mobilised the whole family and asked friends to bring his daughter to her senses.

The effect of this long-distance pressure was soon evident. Not even the Californian sun could bring colour to Christina's cheeks. Her youthful face looked pale and drawn. To find herself the target of so many reproaches and rebukes was a bewildering experience for a girl who had been everybody's darling all her life. The lawyers joined in the chorus of woe explaining that she was financially totally dependent on her father. And what about the Trust? That had already been revised! Twenty-one or not, she would not be entitled to a penny piece.

As the weeks went by the war of nerves intensified with columnists on either side of the Atlantic chipping in with bits of information fed them by interested parties. Christina escaped to a clinic – it was not exactly a break-down – then decided to get away from it all and think things over. She travelled to London, her husband hot-foot in pursuit. He announced that his wife's twenty-first birthday would be celebrated with a tremendous party in Hollywood but, within days, the party was cancelled. Christina returned to the States but not to the Bolker home in Los Angeles. Instead, she stopped over in New York.

When Tina Blandford flew from Europe to meet her the obvious inference was that she was joining the anti-Bolker crusade and had come to persuade Christina to unmake the hasty marriage. They spent many hours closetted in their apartment at the *Regency Hotel*. What has since transpired suggests theirs was a most extraordinary conversation. Tina advised her daughter to end her marriage but told her almost in the same breath that she herself was about to be married again. Christina's marriage was wrong, her own marriage was right. Mother told daughter that she had just spent a fortnight at Quiberon on the French Atlantic coast discussing the future with her intended husband.

Still only forty-two, a young forty-two, with half her life before her, she might have expected Christina to wish her well. But the daughter's response was muted and not only because of the contrast between her own predicament and her mother's plans. The trouble was that Tina's choice had fallen on the man she, Christina, had been brought up to regard as her father's worst enemy. Stavros Niarchos becoming her step-father was an idea difficult to accept.

The dialogue between mother and daughter was one to challenge the inventive skill of a Noel Coward. Had it not taken place against the background of broken homes and broken hearts, conflict and tragedy, it might have been the stuff of situation comedy, separate tables, bedroom mix-ups, change of partners, collision and confusion. Instead it was a sad, sad story.

For a while Christina was still dithering. She rejoined her husband, then left him again. Her mother's affairs were beset by no such complications. At the end of October, 1971, Tina Blandford and Stavros Niarchos were quitely married in Paris. Roger Monnet, Mayor of the eighth arrondisement, conducted the simple ceremony, attended only by Tina's mother, Arietta Livanos, who welcomed Stavros into the family as her son-in-law for the second time. It was she who encouraged this marriage, an example of a Greek matriarch's resolve to keep grief and joy, ships and fortunes within the family.

In the circumstances, the public reaction to the marriage was not surprising. In three crisp lines the Hamburg news magazine *Der Spiegel* summed up the view (which I do not accept) widely held in Greek shipping circles: 'It is assumed in Athens', *Der Spiegel* wrote, 'that the millionaire (Niarchos) only entered into marriage with Tina to protect property. About two-thirds of his fortune belonged to the estate of the late Eugenie.'

The situation was bizarre enough without the running commentary the gossips and the newspapers kept up relentlessly. Not much time elapsed before Niarchos felt obliged to deny a report that he and his wife had quarrelled violently in Monte Carlo – they had not even been in Monte Carlo, he said. More piquantly and accurately, it was predicted that Tina was about to take up residence at the Chateau de la Croe at Cap d'Antibes where she had queened it as Madame Aristotle Onassis twenty years earlier until Niarchos bought the chateau from under Onassis' feet.

The family tangle was beginning to sort itself out. In February 1972, it was announced in Los Angeles that Joseph Bolker, barely six months after his marriage to Christina, had started divorce proceedings against his young wife – under California law it only required a declaration of irreconcilable differences to dissolve the marriage: 'The dissolution of the marriage will permit Mrs Bolker to be reunited with family and friends in Europe,' said an announcement from a Beverly Hills public relations firm. 'The Bolkers each express fondness for the other and each wants the other to be completely happy.'

Their various personal problems solved, at least for the time being, Onassis and Niarchos going their separate ways, could at long last devote themselves to their shipping empires without the distraction of their hectic private lives. Their professional problems were considerable. The shipping boom of the sixties was rapidly petering out.

VIII

KULUKUNDIS OF KASOS

AT three a.m. on a night in August 1968, there was a
knock at the door of the Athens apartment of George
Mylonas, a handsome man of fifty with a swarthy
complexion and grey wavy hair, who was a member of the
pre-Junta Greek parliament and at one time a minister in the
Papandreou Government: 'I knew it wasn't the milkman,'
he said quoting Winston Churchill. When he opened the door
fourteen men crowded in: 'They were all in civilian clothes,'
he recalled.

The fourteen were members of the Greek Security Police.
One of them read out a warrant for Mylonas' arrest which
described him as 'a threat to public order and security'.
Mylonas later admitted that, immediately after the coup which
brought the Colonels to power in Greece in 1967, he and his
friends founded *Democratic Resistance*, an underground organisation. The security officers took him away to a detention centre
whence he was moved to a prison where many of his former
political associates were being held. A week later, they were
all transported to an island, transferred to another and a third
before ending up on Amorgos Island in the Aegean. At the
village of Hora high up in the mountains, Mylonas was
installed in a fortress-like white stone house on high ground.
Though the deportation order under which he was detained
was for six months, he had good reason to fear that worse may
befall: 'I might well have been kept there for as long as the
Colonels were in power,' he said.

The news of his arrest and exile came as a shock to his
daughter Eleni who was living in London with her husband,
Elias Kulukundis, scion of one of the truly great Greek shipping
families from the island of Kasos. A tall, charming, deceptively,

quiet-spoken young man of thirty-one, Elias, though by no means strongly politically minded – his delicately sensitive book, *Journey to a Greek Island*, testifies his love for the country of his ancestors – was not prepared to let his father-in-law rot away on the barren island to which he had been exiled.

As Mylonas had ominously anticipated, when his term of exile ended in February, it was extended to May and in May was extended again. Early in August 1969 when he had been under detention for a year, Elias and Eleni flew to Greece and applied for permission to visit him on Amorgos. Their request was granted and they travelled to the island – Eleni in joyful anticipation of a reunion with her father, Elias determined to explore the territory and the general condition and investigate the possibility of extracting Mylonas from the claws of the Colonels.

Was it practicable? The young couple found George Mylonas unbowed, but circumstances did not encourage high hopes. The detainee was obliged to report at the village police station and sign a register at nine every morning and at six every evening. Policemen and informers were watching his every move. But he was free to walk along the lonely footpaths near the village, one of which took him along the cliff and past a tiny cove whence another path led down to the sea. Supposing he were to start his 'walk' after reporting at six, he could with luck reach the beach within twenty-five minutes. Elias Kulukundis thought up one or two ruses which might put the guards off the scent.

Preparations for a rescue operation were put in hand as soon as Elias and Eleni returned from their visit. The first move was for Elias to smuggle two vital pieces of equipment into Amorgos, one small two-way radio transmitter and one switch with a timing device by which the lights in Mylonas' house could be turned on and off automatically.

The next few weeks were given over to detailed planning which went ahead as methodically as a Simenon adventure. Elias Kulukundis recruited a few Italian helpers who set up headquarters in Rome. The first indication that the ground work was completed reached him in London, when he received a telephone call: 'I have found someone to type your novel,' said the voice using an agreed code. 'She's Italian and very fast.' Elias wanted to know more but the voice sounded impatient: 'I think you should come here and see for yourself . . .'

Two days later he was in Rome. Another week and the 'fast Italian typist', a cabin cruiser capable of ten knots, was ready for her dramatic mission. Elias was studying the map of Amorgos: 'It looks like a yawning whale upside down,' he said. The map showed the south coast to be an almost continuous cliff over a thousand feet high. The sea around the island was known to be the most treacherous in the Aegean. But there was no time to lose. Elias Kulukundis signalled: 'Full steam ahead!'

When the little cruiser set out from Italy on September 19, 1969, it carried six 'tourists', all Italians except for Elias Kulukundis. None of them knew his real name nor the name of the man they were going to rescue. The moment they departed, Eleni, as previously arranged, telephoned her father from London. She knew the police would be listening in: 'That book you wanted,' she said, 'we have sent it and it should reach you soon.'

From that day on, the plan was for Mylonas to stroll to Kyria Aspasia's village café every day at one p.m. to look out for a group of tourists one of whom would be carrying a large book with the title *The Tragedy of Lyndon Johnson* printed in big letters on the black and red cover. It was the signal to tell him that he would be taken off the island that same evening.

The rescue party's trip was not as smooth as planned. The boat was slow and broke down soon after reaching the Ionian Sea. For four nerve-racking days the 'tourists' were forced to cool their heels on Paros Island with the local policeman eyeing them suspiciously. He seemed to be wondering whether he ought to question them but before he reached a decision, the repairs were completed and the six men were on their way.

They sailed through the Corinth Canal without incident and made for Amorgos.

On the second of October, Mylonas arrived at the Kyria Aspasia Café at ten minutes past one and settled down for lunch as usual when his eyes fell on the 'tourists' at a table nearby and on the tell-tale book with the black and red cover one of them was carrying. He hurriedly finished his meal and returned to his house to make the final preparations which he had been rehearsing during the past few weeks. He extracted the time switch from its hiding place and set it for seven-thirty, the time he usually switched on the lights. From his small library he chose a book of poetry, opened it at the page with *The Hymn of Liberty* and put it on the table where the police could hardly miss it when they came to look for him the following morning.

That evening, he went to the police station to sign on half an hour earlier – according to the register this was his four hundred and ninth day on the island. As he turned to go a police officer looked up and said: 'Just a minute!' Mylonas thought the game was up but the policeman went on: 'We've' just received your money," and handed him his 'allowance' which amounted to seventeen drachmas or half a dollar a day.

Keeping a firm control on himself, Mylonas moved away leisurely so as not to arouse suspicion and went on his regular evening's walk, the most momentous excursion in his life. Hidden under his thick sweater he carried a flashlight and the two-way radio transmitter. He was nearing the crucial point where the footpath to the beach branched off when two villagers approached from the other direction, but they just passed the time of day and walked on. Within minutes he was at the top of the path, accelerated to a trot and rushed across the boulders and brambles. For the steep descent he sat down and let himself slide to the bottom a thousand feet below. Within seconds he had reached the beach. He lit the flashlight and set up the little transmitter.

Elias Kulukundis and his associates had made towards an islet some three miles from Amorgos where they waited until it was completely dark, before moving in: 'I was standing at the bow,' Elias recalled, 'and spoke into the microphone of my radio.' Waiting on shore, glued to his receiver, Mylonas heard him say: 'Can you hear me, can you hear me?'

'I can hear you,' Mylonas answered.

'Where are you?'

'On the shore. I have just come down.'

'Shine your light,' Elias asked him.

Though 'not bigger than the flame of a match' the beam was clearly visible. Elias and one of his friends switched to a rubber dinghy and rowed towards the spot where Mylonas was signalling furiously. Even before reaching the shore, Elias jumped into the water, waded towards Mylonas, grabbed him by the arm and helped him into the dinghy. All Mylonas said was: 'Oh, it's you!'

There was no time for Elias to answer. They spent the five longest minutes of their lives propelling the dinghy towards the boat. Mylonas stepped aboard and held out his hands: '*Bon soir, mes amis,*' he said. Elias looked at his watch.

It was seven-fifteen, a quarter of an hour before the police would see the lights go on in the house and assume that Mylonas had returned from his walk. Three hours later the lights would go out again. All went according to plan. By the time the police discovered the disappearance of their prisoner next morning, the rescue launch was over a hundred miles away and heading for Italy. It arrived safely at the point where it had started on its perilous voyage.

A few days later Mrs Mylonas called Amorgos from London and asked to speak to her husband. She was told that he was sick and could not come to the telephone: 'In that case I shall come to Amorgos with a doctor,' she answered. Presently Amorgos called back: 'There is no need to bring a doctor. Your husband is not sick. In two or three days he will be perfectly well.'

Mylonas was flown to London but eventually settled in Switzerland and travelled a good deal organising propaganda against the Greek regime. Elias Kulukundis, his brief political intervention successfully concluded, returned to his desk in London and continued to pursue his literary interests. Other members of the Kulukundis family tried to ignore the episode. It did not seem to disturb their relations with the Junta which were governed by their shipping activities.

A few years before his perilous trip to Amorgos, young Elias Kulukundis, who was born in Britain and spent his childhood in the United States, visited Greece on a vastly different errand. His purpose was to trace the origin of his ancestors and the derivation of his name and look up the few ageing relatives who had not joined the trek of the Kulukundis from their native islands of Kasos and Syros to Athens and the western world. The story is engagingly, beautifully told in *Journey to a Greek Island*.

Kulukundis is a curious name which has kept most of those who bear it busy trying to determine its etymology and its meaning. A household word in shipping the world over – although the firm is better known as R. & K. Lines, which stands for Rethymnis and Kulukundis – the name still evokes puzzled smiles and sounds as strange to Greeks as to the Americans and the English who try to wrap their tongues around it. Even the most strenuous efforts of young Elias Kulukundis to get to the bottom of the mystery did not completely clear it up.

Did the first Kulukundis come from the Kulukuna Hills along the northern fringe of Crete and adopt their name? Was one of Elias' ancestors known as 'Big Kuluki' (Big Dog) or was the first to be called Kulukundis a Turkish slave sailor on an Egyptian ship whose officers amused themselves by tossing coins for the crew to fight over and encouraged them to all sorts of contests? According to the family legend, Elias Kulukundis' great-grandfather was the strongest of the slave sailors who could reach the top of the mast faster than any other, and gathered up all the coins. He came to be known as 'the man who got all' – *Kulu* is Arabic for 'all' – or, the other way round, *Kaluinti* which means 'all that comes to you'. (Years later in conflict with one of his descendants, Aristotle Onassis took up the theme with results which we shall soon see.)

The background of the strange name will probably never be known for sure but, while we are on the subject of Greek names, may I just say a brief word to explain the problem of recurring patronyms which makes it arduous to follow the histories of my Greek friends? Greek islanders, to put it simply, name their first born sons after their own father (first-born daughters after their mothers) with their own names attached. Younger sons are named after their father's uncles, younger daughters after their mother's aunts.

It produces a pattern which is bewildering in its simplicity because the same names keep turning up generation after generation. The Kulukundis family tree starts with the re-doubtable 'Elias of George, named Kulukundis' who named his eldest son George Elias who, in turn, called his son Elias George. The next in line was again George Elias, followed by a new Elias George, whom, incidentally, we encounter in his Anglo-American guise as 'Eddie Kulukundis'.

In one passage of his book, young Elias Kulukundis, the writer, mentions the *Anastasia*, a handsome three-master in which, in 1898, grandfather 'Captain Elias' sailed from his native island of Kasos with a rather unprofitable cargo of roof tiles destined for Russia. With him on board were his wife Eleni, daughter of Manuel Mavroleon from the Peloponnese – the couple's two little boys, six years old George and his four years old brother Basil, and, according to Elias, 'Manuel in his mother's womb.'

The voyage coincided with the rise of Crete against Turkish rule which exploded into heavy fighting and bitter sea battles. Captain Elias was forced to take refuge in the island of Siros with his family and his ship. He had six sons, George Elias, Basil (who died in 1907), Nicholas, Manuel, John and Michael. By the time the fourth son was born the worthy captain's male line had run out of names and the new-born was given the name of his mother's fourth brother, Manuel (Mavroleon).

In the summer of 1970, in the lounge of the Hotel Grande

Bretagne in Athens, home from home to Greek shipowners, the tall, trim elegant Manuel Kulukundis, seventy-one years of age, greeted friends and acquaintances on all sides. Athens was given over to another shipping exhibition and millionaire shipowners were thicker on the ground than at any previous time. Few can match the respect, admiration and affection which the great Manuel Kulukundis commands wherever he goes.

A few weeks earlier, when I tried to contact him in New York where he lives in a permanent suite at the *Pierre Hotel* on Fifth Avenue, he was already on his annual round of the European shipping centres and I only caught up with him in Athens. We settled in a corner of the lounge and the grand old man of Greek shipping collected his thoughts which go back two generations.

Before our conversation rightly started, he asked the waiter for a glass of water ('No, nor mineral water, just plain water'), produced a sheet of paper and a tiny paint box from his inner coat pocket, extracted a small brush, dipped it into the water and, painting as he talked, began to conjure up the outlines of a colourful old sailing ship riding on blue waves. The neat, sure strokes of his brush produced a perfect little watercolour cameo. '*Anastasia*, a Greek Barque', he wrote in one corner and in the other put his signature: 'M. Kulukundis, 1970', and handed it to me. He could not have chosen a more endearing manner of recalling his origins than painting the ship in which he literally sailed into life.

Kasos which Manuel's father left behind when he was forced to take refuge on Siros in 1898 was a peculiar island. It did not have a harbour which was strange enough. Winter gales and trade winds which swept the inhospitable, barren shores made it difficult to approach and sheer poverty drove the young men out – most of them signed on as sailors in Siros, the biggest Greek port in those days. They fought bravely in the recurring wars but lost out when it came to a peace settlement. While other islands were allocated to Greece, Kasos remained under Turkish sovereignty for some time to come.

Buying their cargo in one port and selling it in another (before business expanded and freights were introduced) Kasiot captains traded in Egyptian, French and Italian ports and took their ships as far as the Danube and the Black Sea but were late going over to steam. Only when they banded together in syndicates did things begin to look up but presently World War One was upon them and that really was the end of the Kasiot merchant fleet which was completely wiped out. By 1920, there was not a single Kasos ship afloat. Who knows, but the Kasos captains – most of them living in *xenitin* in Siros – might never have recovered from the blow had they not reared boys like little Manuel Kulukundis: 'I had a great love of ships,' he told me. Ships was all he thought of.

Other youngsters enjoyed stories of cops and robbers, cowboys and Indians. Not Manuel. He had his head buried in the Lloyds' circulars addressed to his father. While Captain Elias was at sea, the boy memorised every shipping deal that had been transacted since 1907. Even at school he talked of little else but ships with an equally interested mate, Minas Rethymnis, like him the son of a sea captain. 'Holidays were spent on father's vessels,' Manuel continued. 'We went as far as Constantinople and the Danube. My ambition was to be a sailor, to get on, get to the top!' The shipping stories which fascinated him as much as adventures at sea, were of purchases and sales of ships.

He still remembers every trip his father made to buy a new ship, recalls Captain Elias travelling to London to find a ship at the same time as Michael Lemos, Costa M. Lemos' father. Captain Elias soon settled on a steamer but Michael Lemos did not find a suitable vessel. With time on his hands, Lemos agreed to sail with Elias Kulukundis as his first mate: 'At that time,' Manuel Kulukundis smiled, 'Costa Lemos was still in short pants.' It is not easy to visualise the mighty Lemos in short pants.

Before the first world war Greek shipping had a stormy passage. The reputation of Greek owners was terrible. Greek ships operated on a shoestring with minimal safety precautions which made them poor security risks. Some Greek owners were as reckless financially, over-extended beyond their resources and so weak that underwriters viewed every transaction with grave suspicion.

Things reached a very low ebb when Dimitri Moraitis, a prominent owner, got into difficulties. His grandfather having pioneered transatlantic liners (*Themistocles* and *Athena*) the grandson continued in his tradition but there was trouble when the Embiricos brothers, cousins of his wife, built trans-atlantic ships in competition with his. There were simply not enough customers. To make matters worse two Moraitis ships went aground within one month and were lost. The under-writers refused to pay compensation and started a chain reaction which affected every Greek shipowner. It lingered for a long time.

Presently, though, the Greek merchant navy was caught in the war, served well and suffered grievously. It was in the war that the path of Captains Michael Lemos and Elias Kulukundis crossed again. In 1917, they were both in Egypt with their ships: 'Our vessel, the *Lily*,' Manuel Kulukundis said, 'was torpedoed off Port Said,' The Lemos ship came to the rescue, took the Kulukundis crew aboard and carried them to safety.

Manuel was with the Greek Navy at Marseilles, was later transferred to Salamis in the Saronic Gulf and served as an interpreter attached to the admiral, but remained in close touch with his old school friend, Minas Rethymnis. Greece was still neutral when Minas' elder brother, Captain Nicholas B. Rethymnis, a gentle six-footer who followed his father as master of the 4,500 ton cargo ship *Chrysopolis*, became involved in what has been described as a mixture of Greek tragedy and Italian comic opera:

'We were sailing through the Mediterranean from Alexandria to Hull with a cargo of cotton seeds,' he recalled, 'when we were attacked by an Austrian submarine.' Some of the crew were killed and he was wounded but when the Austrians made to sink the ship, he protested that she was a neutral vessel, and suggested that they should be satisfied with the cargo which included sixty-three million eggs. At that moment, a British armed merchant cruiser approached and shelled the submarine. Captain Rethymnis used the confusion to get away as quickly as possible.

'Two days later, the submarine caught up with us once more and the whole business started all over again,' he said. An Italian passenger ship came on the scene, the submarine left me, torpedoed the other ship and made off.' Captain Rethymnis rescued a hundred and sixty-five of the ship's crew and passengers and put into the North African port of Derna, then occupied by the Italians. Though he had saved so many lives, the suspicious Italians thought he was in league with the Austrians, impounded his ship, interned the crew and took him to Rome for a court hearing. The case dragged on for a year. It took even longer before the ship was released and he was indemnified for a year's lost trading.

The Greeks thought the British were allocating the most difficult trade to their ships which became easy prey for German U-boats and surface raiders. Over sixty per cent were destroyed, though losses in men were not heavy because few vessels were torpedoed without warning and sailors were able to take to the boats or were picked up by the submarines. No sooner was the war over than Greek shipping was in trouble again. Greek captains who had made a lot of money in the war bought small ships from the Scandinavians, but as soon as the price of ships fell there was an epidemic of losses at sea. Twenty ships went down in quick succession and claims on the insurance companies mounted. Underwriters were highly suspicious.

When a ship sprung a leak and went down, who could say what really caused the loss? Was it not possible that owners sacrificed their ships to collect insurance which was higher than the ships' value? Old ships, highly insured, going down like ninepins – it was bound to create doubts and resentment. Putting it mildly Manuel Kulukundis said: 'There were slurs on everybody's reputation'.

The war over, the Kulukundis family settled in Piraeus but with Greek shipping in the doldrums, Captain Elias sent Manuel to London to try his luck in the centre of world shipping. The young man's allowance was £20 a month, enough to live on and to save a little. He found a job as an apprentice with a leading charter agent, studied the market and kept his ear to the ground. In Southampton Row, he shared a small apartment with his old friend Minas Rethymnis and it was not long before the two young Greeks teamed up as business partners and struck out on their own: 'We put up £75 each to start a shipping office, spending the money on the rent of a single room at 15, Great St Helens, off St Mary Axe, in the City of London, and on furniture.'

The date was July 21, 1921, which marks the birth of R. and K., one of the work's proudest shipping empires: 'Having started with a total of £150,' Manuel Kulukundis said toasting the firm's fiftieth anniversary, 'R. & K. went on to represent eighty ships – as shipbrokers we made £30,000 a year in commission alone.' In the passage of time, the income from ships which Manuel and Minas acquired was much bigger.

What were they worth in the beginning? 'There was no goodwill involved,' said Manuel. 'It was a personal business. Unless we went with it, the value was nil.' There were no more than twenty shipping offices in London at that time – now there are a hundred and twenty. There were as yet no big conglomerates which, as is the practice now, transact business in their offices without recourse to brokers.

Expanding cautiously, Manuel and Minas rented a second room and acquired an office boy who (as we shall see) became one of Britain's wealthiest shipowners. They had to watch the volatile market carefully. Suspicion still clung to the Greeks like a leech. Underwriters contested every Greek claim but right was not always on their side.

Kulukundis cited one instance of a ship belonging to a cousin of Costa Lemos which struck a reef off the Gold Coast (now Ghana) and sank. According to the captain the disaster was caused when the ship's chains broke which made it impossible to stop the vessel. The underwriters distrusted his account and refused to pay compensation. The case went to court where the owners produced a photograph which clearly showed the chain hanging loose – it was broken.

In another case in which the underwriters refused to pay they relied on the evidence of a man who gave the exact time he saw a ship at a certain position. In court, the owners' lawyer asked the man to look at the clock and tell him what time it was. He could neither read nor tell the time. Giving judgement against the underwriters, the judge harshly criticised them and their lawyers.

Yet again, a ship of which Manuel Kulukundis was the registered owner went aground in the Straits of Magellan while the pilot was aboard. The underwriters refused to pay and Kulukundis started proceedings against them which went to the House of Lords ('Manuel Kulukundis v. Royal Exchange Insurance Company'). Kulukundis won.

He quoted these cases to show how underwriters reacted to the earlier epidemic of losses. For a long time Greek ships could not get insurance cover at all. The crisis was only resolved when the shady opportunists were eliminated and reputable owners restored confidence.

IX

ON THE CREST OF A WAVE

SMALL as they were, Kulukundis and Rethymnis came into shipping on the crest of a wave: 'When I arrived in London in 1920', Manuel Kulukundis recalled, 'ships' prices were sky high and a twenty year old ship of 6,000 tons cost £175,000. The boom did not last. The Inter-Allied Commission, headed by Lord Inchcape, took over some two thousand five-hundred German ships which had survived the war and offered them for sale. Such a large number of ships coming on the market quickly depressed prices. Within eighteen months, the value of the £175,000 ship had gone down to – £11,000. The glut had depressing effect on freight rates. Prices dropped all round.'

Manuel Kulukundis' first transaction as a broker was in August 1921: 'I bought one of the ships Lord Inchcape offered for sale, the *Rooke*, built for the Germans in Belgium thirteen years earlier." He paid £17,000 for her. It was the first of hundreds of purchases and sales he negotiated for his clients, for himself and his partner. In 1923 he was appointed London Agent of the Union of Greek shipowners.

While Manuel operated in London, brothers George (who left the Greek Navy) and Nicholas sailed on as sea captains, while the younger brothers, John and Michael continued their studies – John in Athens and Glasgow (engineering) and Michael in Paris. All four eventually joined the firm and are still active partners. So is Minas Rethymnis who brought his brother Nicholas into the R. & K. fold.

The shipping business was as intricate as ever. For three years – from 1923 to 1926 – prices remained low and only began to rise again when the Inter-Allied Commission had no more ships to offer. A new crisis developed in 1927 when a big

Argentinian grain firm, Bunge & Co., of Buenos Aires, demanded a reduction in the cost of insurance – with results that affected all Greek owners. While agreeing to reduce the cost of grain cover the underwriters stipulated that Greek owners should be excluded. A howl of protest greeted the discrimination and only after protracted negotiations were the underwriters persuaded that the reduction should apply at least to some Greeks if they qualified for inclusion in an official 'approved list'.

The arrangement threatened to leave many Kulukundis clients uncovered. Unless their names were submitted for approval – and accepted – their ships could not get charters. In the event, charterers, rather than go through the rigmarole of applying for approval, chose other ships whenever they were available leaving the Greeks out in the cold.

'At the time, we had thirty ships of which sixteen were on the approved list,' Manuel Kulukundis said, 'but as Agent of the Greek Union, it was my duty to protect all Greek owners.' He went to see the Committee of Lloyds and persuaded them to lift the ban in exchange for slightly higher premiums all round. It was a splendid solution but owners already on the approved list objected because they had to pay more and called it 'a black day for Greek shipping'. Manuel Kulukundis faced a great deal of criticism.

'The opposite was true!' he exclaimed. 'It was a good day for Greek shipping!'' In the passage of time the arrangement led to the establishment of a Minimum Rate which he negotiated and which resulted in an overall reduction of rates. It gave Greek owners greater prestige – had their ships not been reliable, the rate would not have come down: "The insurance business was largely operated by Jews.' said Kulukundis, "and they look at every penny.'

By 1929, prices were sixty per cent up and still improving. The future looked bright. Manuel Kulukundis took time off to get married in Paris – to Calliope Hadjilias, daughter of another Kasos-Siros shipowner. They have two sons, one living in London, the other in New York, both in shipping.

Shipping remained extremely sensitive to outside influences. The U.S. Stock Exchange crash escalated into a world-wide economic crisis which hit shipping hard. Money was in short supply, ships were laid up, British banks, which had advanced funds, pressed owners to sell, forced sales became the order of the day and business, as Kulukundis put it, was from hand to mouth.

The black days of Greek shipping before the war were not forgotten. What, if unscrupulous captains in a new crisis scuttled their ships as their predecessors had done? Kulukundis was worried lest there would be new grave difficulties. 'I tried hard to persuade underwriters to reduce insurance of ships under our control to the amount of outstanding mortgages to make it unprofitable for captains to cast away their ships in order to collect insurance. But underwriters who had extracted high premiums for so long would not entertain my suggestion,' he said.

Determined that history should not repeat itself, he issued an ultimatum to underwriters: 'I am giving you a warning in writing that I have asked for a reduction. If anything happens, there can be no arguments and you will not be able to say that the insurance was higher than the value of the ship!' That did the trick. Underwriters agreed to the reduction.

It was only half of the Kulukundis formula to meet the situation. What was required, he argued, was to get rid of old ships as fast as possible and get new ones. The difference between the value of the old ship and a modern ship was small: 'It dawned on me that this was the time to change over.'

He expounded his idea in the Greek shipping journal *Naftika Chronika* (which has since published other policy-forming contributions from his pen), talked to Greek owners and persuaded them to sell their old ships and buy better ones. With prices low and much money owing on ships in operation, it was an obvious move. British experts were doubtful and Lord Runciman gave him a friendly warning: 'Don't sell your ships!' but when Kulukundis explained his scheme, Lord Runciman agreed that it was the right thing to do.

Kulukundis practised what he preached: 'I sold a ship called *M. Poutous*, a 6,000 tonner built in 1900, for scrap and received £2,100 for her,' he said. 'That same month I bought the 8,000 ton single-deck *Maindy Grange*, built in 1914, for £2,150, just £50 more than the proceeds from the *M. Poutous*. With this £50 I bought fourteen years of appreciation and 2,000 extra tons.' Another significant transaction was his purchase of the *Mount Ida* for which he paid £6,000. Two years later he sold her in Germany for £55,000. Within one year Kulukundis made thirty-seven such transactions, half sales, half purchases. Clients were duly grateful. Owners read what he wrote, watched what he did and followed suit. Stavros Livanos did it, the Goulandris and Embiricos families did it, the Oinoussai owners did it.

One of Kulukundis' early clients was Michael C. Lemos who did not have the resources to buy a ship of his own and came to see him with his cousins and friends. Kulukundis organised them into a group and bought ships for them. He enabled Michael's son Costa to participate in the purchase of a big cargo vessel, *The Great City* which cost £14,000, and was eventually sold to the Germans for over £50,000. The Lemos clan finally withdrew from the Kulukundis office, went over to their relative, Marcos Lyras, and took a share in his business: 'Every Greek wants to be his own master,' Kulukundis said. Still, as the years went on, more and more Greeks entrusted their affairs to Manuel's firm and were nursed to wealth and prominence.

In December 1931, Manuel was at his desk in the City of London when he was told that a young man was in the general office waiting to see him. The young stranger introduced himself as Aristotle Onassis and told Kulukundis the story of his life – how he went to the Argentine as a youngster, how he was down and out and wanted to return to Europe, how he went to Buenos Aires harbour and saw a ship called the *Archimedes* whose captain refused to give him a job or take him back to Europe: 'It was a good thing for Onassis,' Kulukundis chuckled: 'because it changed his whole life.' (Forced to stay on in the Argentine, Onassis made money with tobacco deals until he was rich enough to buy ships.)

He came to see Kulukundis about a certain Union Castle Line ship which he had had his eye on when Kulukundis snapped it up. Would Kulukundis sell him the ship now? Kulukundis would not, and Onassis went on to look for ships elsewhere; to Canada where he bought the six frigates which set him on the road to fortune.

Greek shipping expanded by leaps and bounds. In the hectic years between 1921 and 1939, on which Kulukundis left his mark, the Greek tonnage multiplied five times. The outbreak of the second world war put an end to independent trading but, while their ships were quickly recruited, Greek owners were in an unenviable position. After the fall of France, with Britain facing invasion, foreigners were not popular in the threatened island.

'I had a house in Sussex,' Kulukundis recalled, 'and as a foreigner was obliged to report to the police twice a day. It was very irksome.' Like most other Greeks, he took his family to New York. This was the great exodus of the 'London Greeks' who settled in the United States and became the 'American Greeks'. Captain Nicholas Rethymnis also left Britain and went to the United States where he represented R. & K. and eventually became an American citizen.

At the beginning of the war, Kulukundis and the other London Greeks from Kasos (Nicolaou and Hadjilias) and their families controlled a fleet of seventy-five steamers, ten of them new. Another eight vessels were on order for British R. & K. companies which also owned eight second-hand ships. Hardly any of them survived the war.

At that time, the United States were building so many ships that there were not enough sailors to man them. Surely, the surviving Greek crews could fill the gap and resume their war efforts: 'We approached the U.S. Government and offered to serve,' said Manuel Kulukundis who represented the Union of Greek Shipowners in New York as he had done in London before the war. The U.S. Maritime Commission welcomed the suggestion and devised a scheme to employ Greek crews by lease-lending fifteen Liberty ships to the Greek Government in exile.

The arrangement was for these ships to be chartered to the War Shipping Administration and used for transportation as required by the war. 'We created the Greek Shipowners New York Committee to administer them,' Kulukundis said. By 1943 the fifteen ships were in service. The following year they carried supplies for the allied invasion armies across the English Channel and took part in the Normandy landings, the first stage of the liberation of Europe from the Hitler yoke. Several were lost and their crews went down with them.

Greek losses at sea were proportionately higher than those of any of the other allies. To say that the Greek merchant fleet was decimated is an understatement. To all intent and purposes it was wiped out – almost all the Kasiot ships were among the casualties. Faced with the daunting task of resurrecting the Greek merchant fleet with virtually nothing to build on and no money, the New York Committee of the Greeks was groping for a way to save the situation.

It was Manuel Kulukundis who initiated a historic transaction when the United States were left with a large number of Liberty ships and it occurred to him that they could be transferred to the Europeans to replace their losses. His first move in September 1946, was to approach the U.S. authorities on behalf of his Committee, with a request to let them have the Greek-crewed Liberty ships which had survived the war.

With Greece in the throes of a civil war and the Communists fighting to get control of the country, the legitimate government needed help. Cabinet minister, Sophocles Venizelos, son of the late great Elefterios Venizelos, went to the United States seeking a loan to save Greece from the Communists. The U.S. Government hesitated but soon made 400 million dollars available to Greece and Turkey.

'I raised the question of the Greek merchant fleet with Sophocles,' Manuel Kulukundis recalled, 'and persuaded him to go to Washington with me to ask for ships . . .' They went

and saw Admiral Smith of the Maritime Commission and asked
for a hundred Liberty ships to be allocated to Greek owners
who had lost vessels in the war. Admiral Smith was sympathetic. Agreement in principle was quickly reached and the
ships were promised – provided the Greek Government was
prepared to guarantee a loan covering their cost:

'The ships could not be bought for cash,' Kulukundis
explained, 'because there was none.' In the first place, the
Greek Government had to be persuaded to give the required
guarantee. Delicate negotiations between Athens and the
owners were quickly started and helped along by the redoubt-
able Demetrios Cottakis, who has since become the 'Oracle
of Greek Shipping'. They were successful and, once the
guarantee was assured, American credit terms were extremely
generous. One million tons of shipping were involved, the
average price of these 10,000 ton ships was 544,000 dollars.
Cash required was 138,000 dollars per ship and the balance
on credit over twenty years at three and a half per cent interest.

It was not difficult to obtain the cash. While the United
States was pouring supplies into post-war Europe there was no
shortage of cargoes. Once the charter was signed, the banks
advanced the money, the first freight enabled the purchaser
to put down the 138,000 dollars. Continuous employment was
assured. The rest was to be repaid at 25,000 dollars a year,
but earnings were in the neighbourhood of 150,000 dollars
leaving ample funds to invest in more ships and other ventures.

Instead of throwing their hats in the air, many Greek shipowners were doubtful and hesitant. Would this kind of arrangement not make them dependent on the United States? Might
there not be government interference in their operations?
Were the ships good enough? With a hundred or more highly
individualistic Greek owners, objections covered a wider range.
Each had a problem of his own. When freight rates slumped,
before the ships were delivered, some owners threatened to
withdraw their application. There was a grave risk that the
allocation would not be taken up. Other owners, at the same
time, greedily demanded more than their fair share.

'Some Greek owners who returned to London after the war,' Kulukundis continued his account, 'did not want the ships claiming that they were badly built and would quckly fall apart.' Kulukundis travelled to London and tried to change their minds but they would not listen. The Goulandris brothers were sceptical; Livanos and Lemos on the other hand clamoured for ships. Kulukundis applied for a few but, he said: 'Not for as many as we ought to have taken, because we already had twelve, plus a number of Canadian ships.' He acquired fifty-eight Canadian frigates similar to the Liberty ships, and distributed them among friends and associates.

The long negotiations for the first hundred Liberty ships were taken over by their new owners. Fourteen ships were allocated by lottery and the first to come out of the hat was *Hellas* which was won by George Cristos Lemos, shipowner and intellectual, resident in Lausanne. The second was *Ameriki* (America) which went to a company called Marathon S.A.

Two of the ships which Stavros Niarchos and his uncle Koumantaros took over were renamed *Captain Matarangas* and *Captain Papazoglou*, after captains who had lost their lives in action on Niarchos-Koumantaros ships. One owner named his ship *Flight Lieutenant Vassiliadis* after his son who was killed in action with the R.A.F. Stavros Livanos' original allocation was twenty-four ships but other Greeks protested and he was restricted to twelve which he named after the rivers of Greece. Costa M. Lemos named his first Liberty *Michail* after his father – by custom most ships were named after fathers, mothers, sisters, patron saints, but some of the fleets were so big that the owners ran out of relatives.

Only one Liberty, the *Megalochari*, went to a man who had not lost a ship in the war and was not even a shipowner. Textile manufacturer I. Theodoracopoulos got his chance when some of the more conservative Greek owners hesitated and he stepped into the breach. The vessel was the first of many which sailed under his flag.

In addition to the Liberty ships, the Americans offered their

European allies some of their 16,500 T2 tankers, seven of which were allocated to the Greeks.

By this time, Onassis was anxious to get into the act. Already angry because, not having lost any ships in the war, he did not qualify for a Liberty, he staked a forceful claim for the seven tankers. They were the kind of ship he wanted to strengthen his fleet and he felt he was entitled to them because his financial acumen and persuasive powers had helped to break down American reluctance to finance Greek shipping. Some of his compatriots took the view that he only applied for the ships to prevent other Greeks from getting their hands on tankers and finding out how profitable the business was.

It is part of the great shipping legend – possibly a little exaggerated – how he pulled every string he knew, approached the U.S. Government directly, offered them a share of the profits if the ships were allocated to him. Opening up a second front, he circulated an 'Open Letter' to all it may concern in terms which were less than flattering about his fellow Greeks and particularly insulting about Kulukundis who was incensed when a copy reached him. 'I called a meeting of Greek ship-owners to discuss the extraordinary situation,' Kulukundis said, still angry in retrospect. He had no quarrel with Onassis, he added, but he strongly objected to the allegations in the offending communication: 'It was libellous,' he claimed. He and his friends protested to the U.S. Government and demanded that Onassis' own claims should be closely scrutinised.

So violent were the reactions against Onassis that, at one stage, Costa Grastos, his loyal right-hand man, tried to protect him by taking responsibility for the passages which Kulukundis regarded as scurrilous and objectionable. Kulukundis would have none of it: 'I was convinced', he said, 'that the whole letter was written by one and the same man!' Anyway, Onassis repudiated the suggestion that he had put his name to another man's epistle, as if he could not write his own letters.

One passage which Kulukundis regarded as a personal insult harked back on an earlier and entirely friendly conversation between him and Onassis about the origin of the Kulukundis name. It was the occasion when Manuel mentioned the theory – which he did not accept – that his great grandfather Elias, son of George, had been given his name as 'the man who got everything'. Recalling the conversation Onassis maintained that 'by his own admission' Kulukundis meant "a grabber" and "a thief".

Another passage, indicating that Onassis had been nursing a grievance against Kulukundis for a long time, referred to the early twenties when he, Onassis, was anxious to return to Europe from the Argentine. According to him, the captain who refused to take him was one George Kulukundis which went to show how mean a Kulukundis could be! In such belligerent mood, Onassis – or perhaps Kulukundis – must have become confused because there are several inconsistencies in their respective accounts of those distant days. There is a big question mark against the name of the particular ship. Was it *Atlanticus* or *Archimedes*? When talking to me about his attempts to get away from Buenos Aires, Onassis described the captain he approached as a Scotsman, the ship, he said, was called *Socrates* – he could not possibly be mistaken because it was his second name. Be that as it may, the conflict lingered; Onassis and Kulukundis have not made it up to this day.

The shipping transactions between Greeks and Americans also went slightly sour. To comply with U.S. regulations governing foreign control of American ships, a few Greek owners financed their American-born friends whose companies acquired American surplus ships. Although at the time the U.S. authorities did not appear to object to the practice, they later described it as a ruse to evade the regulations and ruled that the ships may be nominally owned by Americans but the Greeks who paid for them called the tune and controlled them in practice.

Onassis, Niarchos and other Greek shipping men were indicted for violations of the law. Criminal proceedings were instituted, Onassis was briefly arrested but the charges were soon dropped and the American Government was content to treat the matter as a civil offence. In the event, Onassis was obliged to transfer his American ships to a trust for his American-born children. Both he and Niarchos paid heavy fines. Kulukundis controlled sixteen American companies all of which were involved in the 'surplus ships affair' and each was fined 7,500 dollars.

In the mushrooming tradition of Greek shipping, Captain Nicholas Rethymnis established his own firm, the Rethymnis Steamship Agency in New York with offices in Broad Street. Already past his eightieth year, he was still doing a regular five-day-a-week stint and could be seen at the crack of down striding purposefully through the streets of Manhattan on his way to his downtown office to be at his desk at seven-thirty a.m. Retire? 'Why should I retire?' he asked as if it was the most unreasonable suggestion in the world. He was, in fact, busy making plans to build new ships. With Manuel Kulukundis, he shares more than a lifetime of running ships. Like Manuel, he paints them, too.

While Kulukundis interests were gravitating towards Britain and Greece, Manuel himself stayed on in the United States and became an American citizen. He rented an apartment at the *Pierre Hotel* in Fifth Avenue at 750 dollars a month and later bought it outright for 115,000 dollars by which time he had to pay 2,750 dollars a month for service and maintenance alone.

His luck deserted him in the early sixties when he became involved in a number of transactions which did not turn out well. The U.S. Government filed a multi-million dollar suit against him alleging that he had failed to provide collateral for 35 million dollars of supertanker mortgage insurance as he had undertaken to do. Both his wife and his son Michael, were named in the suit which ended with the forced sale of several American Kulukundis' ships. The setback has not detracted from Manuel Kulukundis' standing in the Greek community. He remains a venerated figure, a legend in his own lifetime, whose place in the history of Greek shipping is assured.

The London end of the Kulukundis enterprise is largely in the hands of his younger brother John who shares his private

office in the City of London with the eldest of the clan, Captain
George. Both are married to girls of the Diacakis family from
Kasos. John's two sons, Elias and Minas, went to Oxford
University but, while a generous sprinkling of the new generation has already graduated to managerial positions, it is too
early to say whether they too, will follow the trade of their
ancestors.

Some of the young ones have turned their back on shipping
and followed their own inclinations. While Elias Kulukundis,
son of Michael, writes, his cousin Elias Kulukundis, son of
Captain George, is dedicated to the theatre. Elias, who calls
himself Eddie, went to school in New York and Connecticut
before going on to Yale. In 1956, he joined the Kulukundis
office in London and was thrown in at the deep end of shipping.
His first job was to attend to a huge Kulukundis ship-building
programme – two tankers commissioned in Britain, five in
Japan, one in Sweden, one in Yugoslavia, and eight dry cargo
vessels in Holland, Britain and Japan.

Greek shipping offices are family affairs, and five members
of the older generation were involved. Though spread widley
over the globe with residences in Montreal, Bermuda, New
York and London, Manuel and his four surviving brothers
were actively engaged in the project: 'Gradually,' Eddie said,
'four of the young ones came in – Manuel's son, Michael's
son, two sons of Nicholas Kulukundis . . .' All except Eddie
worked on a salary: 'I worked for nothing' he said. As an
only son he was the responsibility of his father who shares in
the firm's handsome profits.

In his heart, however, Eddie was disloyal to the family
trade. He worked hard enough but his spare time was devoted
to the theatre. 'When I opened the paper every morning I
read the shipping news first, then turned to the theatre
column,' he said. Every first night in London's West End saw
him in his place in the stalls. The stage became almost an
obsession and all he wanted – in the vernacular of Greek shipowners – was to 'participate', in other words to put money

into the theatre. A large, bustling, erudite man, he brought an acute business sense to his hobby which has since started to bear rich dividends. When I talked to him in his office in a charming old-fashioned narrow street in London's theatreland, with posters and charts lining the walls, telephones ringing, cables arriving and being drafted, just as in a busy shipping office, he still shuddered at the thought of the days when the theatre's call became irresistible: 'It was frustrating,' he said. 'I knew nobody to whom I could give money' – a fate which can only befall a rich shipowner.

This peculiar difficulty was solved when he met Hobart Moore, the Kulukundis auditor who happened to be Treasurer of the Shakespeare Trust. Moore kindly arranged for Eddie Kulukundis to put money into a minor theatrical production. Eddie was hooked. It was not long before he decided to follow his true vocation. Fourteen years after he first joined the family firm, Eddie Kulukundis left the City. He invested in other productions – theatrical, not shipping – and, in June 1970, set himself up as an independent producer.

The first play he produced in his own right was Jack Pulman's *The Happy Apple* which was favourably reviewed but brought him no great financial reward. His next was Arnold Wesker's *The Friends*, followed by *How the Other Half Loves* (with Robert Morley) which recouped its London production costs of £18,000 within the first seven weeks and opened in New York in March 1971. He crossed the Atlantic again with David Mercer's *After Haggerty* which was a hit in London before capturing big audiences in New York, Before long he was in the big league of producers with two shows in London and one in the United States, running at the same time. The shipping scion who started out as a Maecenas was beginning to make the theatre pay. Although hard-headed, practical Greek shipowners hate to lose their off-spring to any pursuit outside their traditional sphere, they proudly watched the Kulukundis colours fluttering over the English and American temples of make-believe.

* * *

Every morning when John Kulukundis arrives at the big R. & K. London headquarters at St Clare House, a catalogue of the firm's ships with their exact positions and destination, details of the crew, cargo and next assignment is put before him. It makes impressive reading. There are few ports which are not listed as points of departure or arrival – from Baltimore to Aruba, from San Francisco to Rotterdam, from Inchon to Kokura, from Yokohama to New York, from Tyne to Leningrad, from Mombasa to Glasgow, Kulukundis ships criss-cross the oceans. Owned by members of the family whose names adorn their bows, they add up to huge tonnage. At a conservative estimate they are worth some £100 million.

It is a far cry from the £150 with which Manuel Kulukundis set up shop in one room fifty years ago.

X

GREEK OFFICE BOY INTO ENGLISH OWNER

E MERGING from Wellington Barracks, spick and span in their immaculate battle-dress uniforms, the small detachment of the famous Grenadier Guards took up position at Buckingham Palace. The traditional ceremony of the Changing of the Guard, most English of English public spectacles, went across the scene with measured, clockwork precision. The band struck up in the forecourt, the handsome second lieutenant in charge issued a few clipped commands and the new unit was duly installed. Good old England! The young Guards officer's name – Bluey Mavroleon.

Mavroleon is a very Greek name which means Black Lion but possibly derived from an ancestor who was known as *Mavro-Elias* (Black Elias). The young officer was proud of his name but had anyone addressed him in Greek he would not have understood a word. And thereby hangs a long story.

The Mavroleons come from Kassos a small island off Crete whose sailors first carried the Standard of revolt against the Turks in 1821. Their family tree is headed by one Hazimanolis Malliarakis whose wife, for reasons that are lost to conjecture, was referred to as The Virago. The couple's daughter, Marigo, figures in the family legend as Old Yia Yia, a fine needle-woman, renowned for her tapestry, embroidery and lettering – as she was illiterate the letters must have been drawn for her by better educated friends.

Old Yia Yia's husband, Vasilios Mavroleon, was a highly educated merchant and part owner of sailing ships (but no sailor) whose thoroughly documented transactions would have made interesting reading had they not been lost to posterity. Elias Kulukundis who has delved into the family's history, explains what happened to Vasilios Mavroleon's archives: 'Old Yia Yia had an abhorrence of papers . . . After her husband's death, year by year, for the remainder of her life . . . she tore out the pages of the old man's ledgers, fastened them in a little looseleaf binder and hung them on a nail in the outhouse across the courtyard.'

Vasilios and Old Yia Yia Mavroleon had four sons and two daughters, one of whom, Eleni became the wife of Captain Elias Kulukundis. One of the sons, Manuel Mavroleon (1877-1956), became a civil servant in the Greek Ministry of Agriculture and married a girl called Vassiliki Christodopoulos. The eldest of the three sons Basil M. Mavroleon, was born in 1901 in Tripolis in the Peloppenese, the wild and beautiful southern half of Greece, went to school in Athens, studied engineering for a year but left university to take a job as a clerk in the National Bank of Greece.

This 'fantastic job' – considering the state of the country and unemployment in Greece after the first world war – carried a salary of £2 a week and a pension. 'I had no qualifications,' Basil Mavroleon admitted, 'except a little French – no English. Everybody envied me but I did not think myself lucky to get the job. There was no opportunity for advancements. I could never become an expert at anything.'

As other Greeks, he decided to seek his fortune in *xenitia* – in America: 'I weighed things up,' he said, 'and pondered on what openings there were for someone like me without any qualifications. Jobs were scarce, a better one beyond my reach – what chance did I have in competition with people with superior education and degrees?' His reasoning developed along highly sophisticated lines: 'People taking jobs as waiters', he thought to himself, 'were not exactly endowed with science. If I get a job as a waiter, I shall soon be a head waiter, then manager of a restaurant, perhaps manager and owner of an hotel.' In America all things were possible.

But it was not possible to go from Greece straight to the United States. 'The quota was a mile long,' he recalled. It would have taken years to become eligible for an immigrant visa. 'I decided to go surreptitiously as an illegal immigrant and left home making London my first stop.

Poor but ambitious, Basil reached London where he investigated ways and means of smuggling himself into the promised land of the United States. It was not as easy as he had thought. He made little progress, ran out of money and was getting desperate. As a last resort, he turned to his cousin, Manuel Kulukundis, who had just started his shipping business with Rethymnis. The moment could not have been more opportune.

'As it happens, I need some help at the office,' Manuel told cousin Basil. Although the office was only one room, for the young Basil Mavroleon it was a bright prospect except for just one snag: 'I am afraid we can't afford to pay you,' Manuel confessed, 'but I can advance you twenty-five bob a week until things are more settled.' Twenty-five shillings a week, even as a loan, was better than nothing. Basil Mavroleon, aged nineteen, would-be waiter and, hopefully, hotel owner, settled for the job of office boy at the shipping office of Kulukundis and Rethymnis.

Exactly fifty years after the auspicious day, Basil Mavroleon, head of one of Britain's largest shipping companies and owner of a major shipyard in the north of England, received me in a drawing room of his tasteful and opulent Grosvenor Square apartment, with precious carpets, exquisite ornaments and art treasures. Round-faced and Buddha-like but not at all inscrutable, comfortable but vigorous for a man of seventy, he looked back on the beginning of his career with eyes sparkling in happy memory: 'The other day', he said, 'I took the car down to Brixton' – the South London working-class district. It was a pilgrimage into his past. Accompanied by his secretary he went in search of his first London home in the nineteen-twenties – a part of Brixton which has recently attracted a large number of coloured immigrants: 'My home was a taxi-drivers' boarding house behind the *White Horse Inn*. I paid ten shillings a week for bed and tea. There was just a bed and a basin with cold water to wash in the morning. Not much else.'

In those days, he rose at six-thirty a.m. to catch the cheap-fare working-man's train, nibbling at a buttered cheese roll as he hurried to the station He reached the office at eight a.m.: 'I had just three and a half pence to spend on lunch.' It was seven-thirty or eight in the evening before his day's stint was done and he made his way home for tea (dinner): 'I think back on this time with terrible pleasure,' the wealthy Basil Mavroleon mused. Working hours were shorter on Saturdays – from eight a.m. to three p.m.: 'Saturday afternoon I went shopping at the Elephant and Castle where things were cheap.' He bought several tins of Heinz beans at four pence each, one pound of tea and one pound of sugar to last the whole week.

After six months, Basil persuaded his cousin to give him a regular wage. Business was looking up and Manuel agreed to pay him thirty-five shillings a week. It was a big advance, so much so that Basil had second thoughts about going to the United States and decided to stay in England. In his new affluence he looked for better lodgings and moved in with a Greek friend, E. C. Kyriakides, at a boarding-house off Russell Square, run by an Italian woman. (Mr Kyriakides is now head of the big and prosperous Carras shipbroking firm): 'I paid thirty shillings a week for bed, breakfast and dinner – big deal!' It left him with five shillings spending money but his new home was so close to the office he could walk to work and save the fare.

Promotion was on the way. After a year he was promoted, as he put it, from ordinary office boy to chief office boy at a wage of £2 a week. He made good use of his opportunities. The highly intelligent young man used his time with R. & K. to study the business thoroughly, investigating every aspect of the firm's work. 'He was a secretary, really,' John Kulukundis commented. Basil was hard-working, ambitious, and made rapid progress. He might never reach the elevated position of a hotel manager which used to be his target but the position of manager of a shipping office was, no less desirable and it was not long before it was within his grasp.

Soon after Kulukundis and Rethymnis branched out into their second room across the corridor, Basil Mavroleon became a partner in their broking business with a fifteen per cent share of the profits. For the time being, his bosses – partners really – did not take a penny out of the business but when the profits reached £1,000 a year, they voted themselves a salary. Basil's share was £150.

Trends were favourable, progress swift and before long the little R. & K. offce became the Mecca of Greeks who flocked to London to set themselves up as shipowners. Many of those whom Manuel Kulukundis nursed in these early days have since become very big babies indeed. Basil Mavroleon prospered with the firm. He was already living in a better class boarding-house in Lancaster Gate, when he fell in love with an English girl, Violet Withers, the same age as himself. In 1924 they were married at the Aghia Sophia, in Moscow Road.

Basil bought a little detached house in Wembley Park: 'An adequate house with four bedrooms, dining-room, sitting-room, bathroom, kitchen, garage and little garden.' The price was £1,725 of which he put down £200, the rest on mortgage with annual repayments. Another acquisition was an almost brand-new Lagonda which he bought for £425 from Jack Billmeir, who became the head of the big Stanhope Shipping Company.

In April 1927, Basil and Violet had a little boy who was christened Manoli (Manuel). An old Greek aunt who came to see the new arrival gave him the pet name of Manolui which the boy could not pronounce properly. Hard as he tried, it came out as Bluey and the name stuck: 'I did not think Manoli sounded so good in English, anyway,' Bluey Mavroleon explains. He has been known as Bluey ever since. Eighteen months later a second boy was born and christened Nicholas.

Basil's two younger brothers, Dimitri and George, followed him to London (George was trained in the Nautical College, *H.M.S. Worcester*), also went into shipping and did well. His only sister married a shipowner. Though Basil enjoyed family life, his hobby was work. Much sooner then even he expected, he was appointed one of the managers of R. & K. Still on fifteen per cent of the profits, he was earning between £1,500 and £1,800 a year. The firm moved to bigger premises in Holland House behind the Baltic Exchange. Among the Greek owners who were clients were Lemos, Pateras, Hadjilias, Margaronis, Eustathion, all top-liners. Time came when Basil managed as many as one hundred and ten ships under the R. & K. umbrella. By 1929, he was a member of the Baltic Exchange and a director of R. & K. That year he became a naturalised British subject.

As soon as they were old enough, Bluey and Nicholas were sent to Wellesley House prep. school which turns out impeccable pukka upper-class Englishmen. They were still small boys when their father introduced them to the big shipping centres in the north of England. They visited docks and went aboard the firm's ships whose long-serving crews watched them grow up – shipping in these days was much more of a family affair than it is now, generations of sailors serving generations of owners. The boys were thoroughly anglicised with no hint of their Greek background. Basil Mavroleon himself loved England with the affection of a convert. Without sacrificing his Greek associations, he became English in thought and manner, if not in accent. His Englishness did not only mould his sons; even while he continued in harness with Kulukundis and Rethymnis, it determined his conduct of the business.

'I wanted to have British ships,' he said looking back to the mid-thirties, 'and persuaded my cousins to create a separate shipping firm, Counties Ship Management Company.' With a down payment of £2,000 which he borrowed from Lambert Bros., the English brokers, he bought the new company's first ship, an 8,000 tonner which cost £10,000. Next he asked William Deacons Bank for a loan of £5,000 – 'It took me a month of Sundays to get it' – and put the money down on a series of ships, all named after London districts and English counties: *Mill Hill*, *Pembroke Hill*, *Putney Hill*. At the same time the Mavroleons graduated to an apartment near the West End of London.

'I believed in the future of the British flag.' Basil Mavroleon said somewhat wistfully, 'I believed in a well organised industry but conditions were adverse. I would be far better off, had I gone over to a flag of convenience.' The satisfaction of operating British ships could not banish the nagging thought of what might have been had he followed the example of Onassis, Niarchos, Livanos and all the other flag of convenience merchants whose assets and profits, unburdened by British taxation, overtook his, which is not to say that he is short of the odd £10 million . . .

When war broke out, the 'Counties' ships sailed under the British flag. Basil Mavroleon himself would not desert Britain or join the exodus of the London Greeks who transferred their activities to New York for the duration. In 1939 he took his wife and sons to the United States in the R. & K. cargo ship, *Master Elias Kulukundis*, left his wife in New York and the boys in a boarding school in Toronto before returning to war-time Britain. With John Kulukundis, the only other member of the family to stay behind, he took charge of R. & K. in London. The firm's ships which were not working for Britain were chartered to the Swiss.

Shipping business called Basil Mavroleon to the United States once or twice in the first two years of the war, hazardous trips in a flying boat, starting out from Bristol, first stop Lisbon, then by a circuitous route to dodge the Luftwaffe. On both occasions he visited his sons in Canada. In 1942, when Bluey was fifteen, Basil thought it was time for the family to return to Britain. Violet, Bluey and Nicholas joined the R. & K's *Eleni Kulukundis*, on charter to the Swiss and carrying grain and Red Cross supplies for allied prisoners of war in enemy hands. Surface raiders and U-boats infested the sea as the *Eleni Kulukundis* steered a dangerous course across the Atlantic.

Huge Swiss flags were painted on both sides of the vessel and, as a neutral ship, she sailed with all her lights blazing. The sea was littered with wrecks but there were no signs of survivors. Tucked away in the ship's hold, Bluey and Nicholas were not told when hostile vessels loomed on the horizon.

Other ships were stopped and searched but the *Eleni Kulukundis* completed the voyage without incident. Blissfully impervious to danger the boys thought of the whole expedition as a great adventure. They reached Lisbon safely and flew on by Clipper flying boat to Poole in Dorset.

For the rest of the war the Mavroleons lived at their house in Marlow by the river Thames. Bluey went to Charterhouse public school until December 1944, when, at the age of seventeen, he volunteered for service with the British Army. He was called to the colours the following January and joined the crack Grenadier Guards. Before he could see action, the war in Europe came to an end. Commissioned as second lieutenant, one of his first assignments was public (guard) duty at Buckingham Palace. With his battalion, Lieutenant Mavroleon was posted to Berlin, the Ruhr and France.

Basil Mavroleon was busier than ever, his annual income now in the region of £15,000 to £18,000, more than ten times his earnings in the late twenties: 'For the first six to twelve months after the war', he said with characteristic gusto, 'we enjoyed ourselves.' So as to leave no doubt about his kind of enjoyment (though I might have guessed) he added: 'We rebuilt the business, replaced vessels lost in the war and bought more ships!'

While the Kulukundis brothers (except John) remained in the United States and looked after the Greek end of the business, Basil pursued new ventures in London: 'I came to the conclusion that I should go into tankers. There was a world shortage, and there were literally no British-built tankers under the British registry.

He launched a new company: 'In 1948,' he said, 'I pulled all our various British single-ship companies together in L.O.F.' – London and Overseas Freighters, with headquarters in two patrician buildings in London's Mayfair – 'and placed contracts for five 16,000 ton tankers with the Furness Shipbuilding Company, later bought by Charlie Clore,' he said. It was a difficult transaction which required an investment of close to £4 million but Mavroleon could not get credit.

Furness even asked him to pay in advance: 'They did not trust anybody,' he recalled sadly. Furness did not trust Greeks because they remembered 1918, the end of the first world war when there were so many cancellations that they lost a great deal of money: 'Unlike my cousins in the United States, I could not get a sausage. I had to pay on the nail!' Undaunted, he set about raising the money: 'I had some war risk insurance and I borrowed from the banks. I chartered the ships and sold the dry-cargo vessels – all profitably.'

When Bluey was demobbed in 1948, he and his brother visited Athens. It was their first glimpse of Greece whose classic features were distorted by the civil war. The land of their father was in a sorry state: 'It was a sad place,' Bluey thought. 'I felt strange.' His brief visit did not forge a link with the past. Nicholas stayed for six months to learn the language: 'He was probably closer to Greece than I.'

Later that year, an apprentice by the name of Martin joined the *Lulworth Hill*, one of the R. & K's 'Counties' ships bound for the Argentine on a four-month round trip. The young sailor scraped the hull, chipped decks, shovelled coal, did watch duty. He worked hard. The crew came to like the personable fellow whose real identity was known only to the captain.

Not until the ship reached its destination and his real name was discovered on the official crew list did his secret leak out: 'By this time' said Bluey Martin-Mavroleon, 'the crew knew me well enough not to suspect, as they might well have done in the beginning, that I could be a spy for the owner.' Bluey working his fingers to the bone of a cargo-ship – what a contrast from his elegant existence as a Grenadier Guards officer! 'I enjoyed it,' he said.

Meanwhile Nicholas, his brother, went to Le Rosey, the aristocratic school in Gstaad, Switzerland, which counted the Duke of Kent, Prince Karim Aga Khan and princes from a dozen countries among the pupils. Bluey perfected his French in Paris, where he learned a few other things as well. He had a very good time.

Things were as lively when he returned to London where – not unusual for an ex-Guards officer and son of a wealthy father – he became a fixture on the social scene. Fast cars, night-clubs, skiing excursions to the Continent, beautiful women were the paraphernalia of his young life.

Father was married again. His new wife Janey Trapani who had been married before to an Italian industrialist, had an extremely attractive daughter, Anita, who was welcomed into the Mavroleon family. A substantial shipowner in his own right, Basil Mavroleon soon acquired the status symbols of success, a palatial apartment in Grosvenor Square, a racing stable, stud and model farm – his Marlow estate became a showpiece – and a yacht, *Radiant*, which he bought from Lord Iliffe for £25,000: 'I chucked out the engine and made other adaptations,' he said. When he totted up the final cost, it came to £220,000. *Radiant* was eventually sold for £300,000 to Ghana's luxury-loving leader the late Kwame Nkrumah who had to leave her behind when he was ousted. The yacht is still in Ghana.

For Bluey, it was time to start work in earnest. Though his only experience with ships was his voyage to the Argentine and the incessant shipping talk at home, he was despatched to the Furness shipyards at Middlesbrough, not the gayest of English cities, to supervise the building of his father's first post-war tanker, the 16,325 *London Pride*, and sailed with her on her maiden voyage to the West Indies. On charter to Shell, she loaded oil in Curaçao and sailed to New York where Bluey disembarked. When he returned to London he was put to work in the Marine Superintendent's Department which deals with chartering and operations. Brother Nicholas set himself up in the City as broker and agent and looked after the family's foreign ships.

Not many years elapsed before Nicholas announced his engagement to Patricia Miesegaes, a Dutch girl, as pretty as a picture – even Pietro Annigoni who painted her could not improve her beauty. When they had a baby daughter, Virginia Elizabeth, grandfather Basil Mavroleon bought her a diamond and sapphire necklace for £13,000. To make sure that baby Virginia would not be wanting, he gave her a tanker as a christening present. A year later when Nicholas and Patricia had a second daughter he repeated the performance.

Then it was Bluey's turn. In 1956, he married Gioconda Gallardo from Mexico and did not keep Basil waiting long for new grandchildren deserving of his tankers. Bluey and his wife had two boys, Carlos born in 1958, and Nicholas, born two years later, both of whom followed their father to Wellesley House from which Carlos has since gone on to Eton. Basil's step-daughter Anita married Charles Longbottom, a Conservative Member of Parliament sitting for York.

The whole family were racing enthusiasts. Basil gave his brother Dimitri a horse called *Cephalonian* which won six races within two years. A gay couple, Dimitri and his Spanish-born Maria enjoyed life to the full but in 1956 tragedy struck. They were motoring in Europe when they were involved in an accident. Maria Mavroleon was killed.

Basil steered his ships astutely through the capricious seas of the business and constantly expanded his interests. In 1958 he went into shipbuilding on his own account and bought the Austin & Pickersgill shipyard in Sunderland: 'There were two yards, one for very big ships and a small one,' Basil told me. 'When I examined the situation. I found myself faced with the unpleasant prospect of having to shut down the smaller yard.' He did not want to shut it down – on the contrary! To keep it going until things improved, he dipped into his own pocket, put up £400,000 and, combining business with pleasure, placed an order for a new 600-ton luxury yacht.

Having put the work on his new yacht in hand, he turned his attention to a project of greater magnitude. With support from a group headed by merchant bankers Philip Hill, he launched a new shipping venture, London and Overseas Tankers (L.O.T.), based on Bermuda. He ordered tankers from Dutch, Swedish and British yards (Furness) and, while he was at it, also decided to increase L.O.F's tanker tonnage. In one fell swoop, he commissioned eleven new vessels at a total cost of £22 million and this was only the beginning. The Bermuda fleet, he said, was as yet in its infancy. None of the new ships was in the super tanker class about which Basil Mavroleon had reservations. Before committing himself to bigger vessels, he wanted to see whether they would prove their worth.

The new company was so organised as to give him the best of both worlds. While the Bermuda register provided all the tax benefits of a flag of convenience country, his ships could still fly the 'Red Duster', the flag of the British Merchant Marine which was dear to his heart. Inevitably, the new venture turned public attention to Mavroleon's financial operations. Experts liked what they saw and his enterprises received a rare accolade. 'If you had put your money in L.O.F. early in 1956', a London financial correspondent wrote in July 1957, 'you would show a threefold profit today.'

There was consolation of sorts for those who had missed this raging tide of profits when Basil added a rider: 'I predicted that we would enjoy highly profitable employment in the years 1956, 1957, 1958 and 1959', he said, 'and I have been proved right. But the next three years may not be so profitable. A tremendous number of tankers on order will be coming up for delivery. However, as all tankers will go out of service after that, conditions will again improve.'

Another Mavroleon building programme did not fare as well. Through one of his companies he acquired a house in Hyde Park Gate, opposite Sir Winston Churchill's London residence. His plan was to pull it down and build two houses in its place, one for each of his two sons. The idea misfired. The younger Mavroleons were most grateful but . . .: 'We don't want to live in each other's pockets,' they said politely and declined their father's offering. Sadly, he sold the house at a profit.

His yacht was completed in 1961. With a gleaming white hull and most up-to-date technical equipment ('Like the *Queen Mary* only more modern') she was a gem of a ship. Janey Mavroleon helped to design the sumptuous six double state-rooms, each with a big bathroom. Her own bed was a luxurious brass four-poster, her husband's a copy of a bed Napoleon slept in. With a crew of twenty-four, maintenance and running costs were estimated around £50,000 a year. For a while, Basil Mavroleon, a businessman first, toyed with the thought of offering her for sale but, seeing the yacht in all her glory, Janey would not let him part with her.

The owner's wife performed the launching ceremony and named her *Radiant II*. At the launching party, Basil rather than toast her in Champagne, quoffed beer with the three-hundred workers who built her. As a shipowner and ship-builder, he said, he was proud of *Radiant II*. It was the most splendid day of his life. To a reporter he made a typically un-inhibited statement: 'Some people seem to be ashamed of being millionaires. I am not. Why should I be?'

His enthusiasm was infectious. One of the Sunderland shop stewards penned a calypso, less remarkable for the poetry than for its sentiment, a unique tribute to a shipowner from a shipyard worker. Recalling that the berths at the dockyard had been silent and the workmen on the dole until the new yacht was commissioned, the calypso continued:

'One word I feel that I must add before my poem ends,
　It's appreciation to my most special friends,
　To Mr Mavroleon and his wife, I'd like to give a toast,
　That they may have throughout their lives the things they
　　love the most."

On the way to Monte Carlo – 'She is going to knock them for six' the owner predicted – *Radiant II* called in at St Katherine's Dock in London where he showed her off to his friends and promised to encourage fellow-millionaires to build similar yachts to keep the Sunderland shipyard busy. It was a public relations exercise par excellence.

Basil Mavroleon had good reason to be proud of his yacht. Flying the 'Blue Ensign', for which the owner qualified as a member of the Royal Thames Yacht Club, *Radiant II*, in all but size, compared well with *Christina*, the Onassis floating palace, and the Prince of Monaco's smaller *Deo Juvante*, alongside whom she anchored in Monte Carlo Harbour. The Mavroleons went on a cruise in the Mediterranean and the Aegean, Basil scurrying around the deck bare-foot and bare-bodied while his wife and step-daughter lived up to the family reputation for elegance.

Back at work in London, Basil Mavroleon, elder statesman of shipping, wrote for trade journals and spoke up strongly in defence of British shipyards: 'In spite of the wailings of the misinformed', he said on one occasion, 'most British shipyards are efficient and can compete with any other in the world in quality, speed of production and price.' His own yard, Austin & Pickersgill, made a record profit. Still, as he had predicted, shipping moved into a less prosperous phase. In the early sixties economies became necessary and, going with the times, Mavroleon laid up *Radiant II* barely a year after she was completed. When it became known that he might be prepared to let her go, there were several offers, but no sale materialised.

In November 1962, the crew, many of them in his employ since the days of *Radiant I*, were paid off but most of them were found jobs in his other ships: 'It's not that I'm broke,' he said. He no longer felt justified in paying out £50,000 for two months' pleasure in a year. Instead *Radiant II* started to make money for him. Operating out of Piraeus she was chartered to Charles Wrightsman, the American oil magnate, and later to Lord Marks, head of Marks and Spencer. Chartering yachts is a costly luxury – *Radiant II* could not be hired for less than £4,000 a week. Still the owner had not done with her yet. When the charterers departed, he took her over again for a month's cruise with his family. It looked as if he could not bear to be separated from her.

There was a separation in the family, though. Bluey's marriage broke up and he obtained a divorce from his Mexican wife. Named as co-respondent was Italian Count Guiseppe Ascanio Cicogna whom she eventually married. Two years later Bluey was involved in another romance. Friends had little doubt that Camilla Paravicini, the attractive, twenty-two year old granddaughter of a former Swiss ambassador in London, would soon become his second wife. Another link between Greek shipping and English literature was in the making. Camilla's other grandfather was Somerset Maugham.

For a few brief winter months, the young couple went their own ways. Bluey took part in a motor rally across Morocco, and Camilla went to the U.S.A. When they were reunited in London, Camilla's mother threw a party for a hundred friends to celebrate their engagement. They were married at Henley Register Office, followed by a religious ceremony at the Greek Cathedral in Paris which posed a problem for bride and bridegroom. The ceremony was, of course, conducted in Greek and neither of them understood a single word.

Greek for Yes being *Nai*, complications were only avoided by meticulous preparation. Instead of saying 'Yes, I will', the young bride made her marriage vows with a firm *Nai*! Relations between Camilla's mother Lady John Hope and grandfather Maugham were strained. Nevertheless, when Camilla had a daughter, she was named Syrie after Maugham's late wife. Syrie soon had a little sister, Sacha.

Though still looking ten years younger than his age, Basil Mavroleon was taking things a little easier. He gave up his work for R. & K. and vacated the post of L.O.F.'s general manager. Bluey took over – father and son, both sons, working in close harmony. Unable to leave shipping alone, Basil kept an office in the L.O.P. headquarters and though he divested himself of other interests, still goes there most mornings.

Racing, too, lost its attractions. It was a long time since he had last seen one of his horses run – even when one of them, Deamon, started second favourite in the Derby he did not go to Epsom but went cruising instead. In 1965, after twelve years as a racehorse owner, he offered his stud for sale at Newmarket where the first batch, five mares and three foals, fetched over £50,000. He also sold *Radiant II* – not that he let her go outside the Mavroleon orbit. The new owner was a Liberian company belonging to his sister.

Five years later it was really 'Farewell' to his beloved yacht. *Radiant II* was finally put on the market to all comers. Basil Mavroleon – his sister's company – let it be known that a price of a million pounds would be acceptable. After a year of financial skirmishes and some hard bargaining a purchaser was found at a price not far short of £600,000. The man who bought her – the man able to afford her – was Achilles Frangistas another Greek shipowner. For Basil Mavroleon there would be no more yachts: 'It would take three years to build a new one,' he said a little wistfully, 'I'm seventy, and what's my life expectancy?'

With R. & K. celebrating its fiftieth anniversary, the firm's first office boy settled down to the life of a wealthy English gentleman. At the same time, the magnetism of his Greek heritage began to attract his very English son. Bluey Mavroleon started to attend Greek lessons at Berlitz School and his wife took lessons from a Greek lady: 'I thought it was a great pity that I had not learned Greek at an early age and was so far removed from my Greek origins,' Bluey said. 'I want to keep in contact. The older I get, the more I feel drawn to Greece.'

The younger generation also felt the pull of the ancient country: 'My children are mad about Greece,' Bluey said with evident pleasure. But their English background was much in evidence. One of the family photographs behind his desk, shows his younger son Nicholas resplendent in the gleaming red coat of the Guards.

L.O.F. vessels carry the English message of the Mavroleons across the seas. Most of them have names which leave no doubt about their base – *London Confidence, London Harmony, London Independence, London Pride, London Explorer, London Pioneer, London Prestige, London Resolution, London Tradition, London Advocate, London Banker, London Citizen, London Craftsman, London Statesman* (with *Mayfair Splendour* the only variation on the theme). There is something very personal about these names.

A recent Position List of tankers and bulk carriers owned or managed by Mavroleon records the freights (oil, bauxite, steel, coal, grain, iron ore, scrap) they carry for British Petroleum, Shell, the British Steel Corporation and others from La Plata to Karachi, from the Persian Gulf to Glasgow, from Skaramanga to Baltimore . . . Under the flag of Britannia, Mavroleon rules the waves.

XI

JOHN, JOHN, JOHN, JOHN AND JOHN

THE handsome Aegean island of Andros, which covers no more than twenty by ten miles, has 17,000 inhabitants, a small museum, pleasant hotels, an old Venetian fortress and hot, health-giving springs. It is also the native island of the Goulandris clan which, like most Greek shipping families, only more so, is not easily separated into individual units. Listening to Greeks talking about the current Goulandris generation, the names which crop up are Megaleas, Big John, Hirohito (or 'Nasser'), Strauss, and Son of the Widow. Without these nicknames it is virtually impossible to distinguish the five grandsons of the family's founder, John Goulandris, who as is customary, has bequeathed his Christian name to the first-born sons of his own sons.

Old John Goulandris had five sons, Petros, Basil, Nicholas, Leonidas and Michael, the fathers of the five contemporary Johns – John P., John B., John N., John L., and John M. John P. owed his name to his massive figure – *Megaleas* means the big one. John B. almost as imposing, became known as Big John and John N. as Hirohito because of his slit eyes. When he carried out a 'revolution' against the family and went into business on his own, his nickname was changed to Nasser. John L. is so intensely interested in music that his friends refer to him only as Strauss and John M., whose father died when he was very young, has been known as Son of the Widow ever since.

The names are so confusing that Doris Lilly who tried to unravel the background of the Goulandris clan (which she really thought 'the easiest' to sort out) became completely mixed up and credited John Goulandris with only three sons and even those in the wrong order. The surviving Goulandrises smile indulgently because, in the tradition of the pukka Greek shipowners (and in contrast to the 'parachutists'), they jealously guard their privacy, but are less successful in this respect than with their shipping operations.

Most of the publicity which the name attracts, concentrates on Maria Goulandris, widow of John P. (Megaleas) and what's more, sister of Costa M. Lemos – in shipping terms nobody can boast a more formidable pedigree. The undisputed queen of Greek shipping, Maria Goulandris lives up to her status. A popular hostess whose main base is an apartment in Fifth Avenue, New York, next door to her brother's American pull-up, she is a founder member of the jet set making the rounds of Miami, Paris, London and Nassau, particularly Nassau, where her parties at Lyford Cay attract the upper crust of the 'beautiful people'.

It was at one of Maria's parties at Lyford Cay that her son Peter and Christina Onassis formed their friendship of which their families had such high hopes and which came to an end when Christina embarked on her short-lived marriage to Joseph Bolker. The Goulandris family had the consolation of seeing Peter's name disappear from public gaze into which his romance had thrust it.

The Goulandris family could not hope to escape attention for long if only because their luxury yachts which dot the oceans like diamonds in a vast emerald setting are followed with a good deal of interest. If it was not the *Triaima* (owner, John N. Goulandris), it was the *Anemos* (Alexander N. Goulandris), the *Paloma* (Basil P. Goulandris), or the *Vagrant* (Nicholas P. Goulandris) whose course was avidly tracked – the owner's antecedents will become clearer as we go on. Among Greek shipping magnates, no other tribe boasts a comparable armada of floating palaces for private use. The upkeep of the yachts alone absorbs more than half a million dollars a year, year after year, a measure of the family's wealth.

From the sea to the race track! One public spectacle in which the name of Goulandris figured prominently, was the French-trained filly, *Monade*, winning the Oaks at Epsom –

and £18,000 – for George Goulandris in one of the most stirring hair-breadth finishes of modern racing history. It took two photographs and fifteen minutes of deliberation among the judges to produce the decision. When it was announced, George Goulandris cried with joy.

A Goulandris is liable to shed tears of joy even when spending money, as witness the younger Basil Goulandris who bid 297,000 dollars for a Gaugin still-life at a Paris art auction and clinched the sale. Nothing competitive about his bidding, Basil avowed: 'I wanted a Gaugin, so I bought one'. Just like that! It now hangs by the side of other art treasures in his apartment on Fifth Avenue which is to New York Greeks what Grosvenor Square is to their London compatriots.

While Goulandris exploits in society, sport and arts occupy the headlines, Goulandris shipping operations, however gigantic, are taken for granted. Only a brief notice heralded the launching early in 1971, of the *Andros Orion*, yet another mammoth (230,000 ton) tanker of the Petros Goulandris Sons Group. There was no mistaking the new vessels' association with the Goulandris fleet because her name combines that of the family's native island with that of their firm, Orion Shipping (known in England as Capeside Steamship Company).

Let us, then, try and bring order into this conglomeration of shipping, race tracks, art sales, yachts and sailing contests, matrimonial and business affairs, triumphs and disasters of a family which, at the last count, numbered thirty-eight, including children but excluding ex-wives and ex-husbands, and which, at a conservative estimate, is worth something in the region of £500 million. The eldest of John Goulandris's sons, Petros J., married Chryssie Dambassis, of another Andros shipping family, whose considerable dowry enhanced the family holdings. Petros J. died during the first world war leaving a small shipping business to his son John P. (Megaleas). Having lost his ships in the war, Megaleas started up again in the United States in partnership with brother-in-law Costa M. Lemos. They called the new firm, Triton Shipping and Trading Company.

Even before brother-in-law assumed sole control of Triton (with sister Maria participating), Megaleas launched another company, Orion Shipping, the giant among the family's enterprises, which managed more ships than either Onassis or Niarchos. The Goulandris fleet included thirty-six of the controversial American surplus vessels and was inevitably caught up in the notorious surplus ships affair which played havoc with Greek-controlled shipping in the United States. After protracted negotiations, the family paid 2.5 million dollars in settlement of the Government's claims. Megaleas did not live to fight this battle to the end. In 1950, he collapsed and died at Le Bourget Airport, Paris, leaving a major share in Orion to his widow Maria and their son Peter who joined the firm's management.

Megaleas' younger brother, Costa P. who served with the U.S. army in the war before transferring to the Greek Navy, was closely associated with these shipping operations which he backed up with the fortune of his wife, the former Hebe Lakadoukis, daughter of an Egyptian multi-millionaire, who started her voyage into matrimony with a dowry of half a million pounds sterling in solid gold coins. Costa P. lives in the Hotel *Plaza Athenee* in Paris, indulging his hobbies. His first love is horses and gambling.

The stories circulating about Costa's gambling exploits are unending, if not all accurate. His losses on French race tracks were said to have run into hundreds of thousands of pounds over the years until 1967 when he staked £50,000 on a race on the *Tierce* system which requires the punter to name the first three horses in a race in the correct order. Costa stood to win £550,000 – and his forecast proved correct. He was not paid.

The *Tierce* administrators claimed that the favourite who was soundly beaten had put up a poor performance which became subject to a steward's inquiry. But when the horse ran as badly the following week, this excuse could not be maintained. Instead, the administration alleged that Costa had broken the rules of *Tierce* betting under which no person is allowed to place more than thirty bets on any given combination – Goulandris appears to have placed seventy-one bets. The *Tierce* people admitted that, as a heavy punter, he had in the past been allowed to place more than thirty bets as a special concession but in this particular race was said to have overstepped the mark – and never mind that they had previously turned a blind eye on his over-betting when he was losing! For a time legal actions threatened – against Goulandris for over-betting, against the *Tierce* for refusing to pay – but the end was a secret settlement in which, it is thought, the £50,000 stake was returned to the wealthy punter.

Megaleas' brother, George P., married to an English girl (and divorced), is the art collector; Basil P., caused a family rumpus by marrying a divorcee who soon made her mark in American society with her fabulous parties aboard Basil's yacht *Paloma*; while Basil's twin brother, Nicholas P., owner of *Vagrant*, enjoys yachting as a sport. Their only sister, Dotar whose first husband was an Embiricos (of another noted shipping family), recently married for a second time and outside shipping. Which brings us to the end of the Petros J. line whose frenetic and diverse social activities earned them the reputation of playboys but did not stop them building up one of the world's outstanding shipping enterprises.

The elder statesman of the Goulandris family, only son of old John Goulandris still alive, is Basil J. Goulandris who keeps a shrewd, old-fashioned eye on the business. Rarely venturing far from his permanent suite at the *Ritz* Hotel in London he leaves the day-to-day work to his two sons, John B. ('Big John'), married to Olga Embiricos, and a first-class yachtsman with considerable racing accomplishments at Cowes; and Dino B. who lives in Grosvenor Square, naturally. Their sister Violanda married into a family to which her brother is already linked– she is Mrs Nicholas Embiricos.

Another of old John Goulandris' sons, the late Leonidas J., concentrated on passenger ships and founded the Greek Line. His eldest son, John L. ('Strauss') married to Greek tobacco heiress Aliki Papastratos, branched out with his own company, Ormos (Greek for 'Port'), a passenger line whose prestige ship is the 30,000 ton *Olympia*, first to link Greece with the United States after the war and still going strong. His sister Sandra married into another Andros shipping clan, Cambanis.

John M. ('Son of the Widow'), last of the original John's senior grandsons, is the only one who has remained loyal to Greece with his shipping interests which are based on Athens. His house in Ekali, near Kifizia, is one of the costliest in the world. The trees in the grounds were imported and planted with the help of helicopters – the whole exercise is said to have cost over a million dollars.

Apart from the vagaries of the trade, Goulandris shipping operations, scrupulously and efficiently conducted, were enviously free from complications. But disaster, when it struck, came with shattering force. It was in the early hours of Monday, December 23, 1963, that a cryptic message reached the London H.Q. of John L. ('Strauss') Goulandris: LAKONIA ON FIRE. The firm's officials were roused from their beds and hurried to the office.

According to the records the position of the *Lakonia*, on her Christmas cruise to Madeira and four days out of Southampton, England, was about 140 miles north of her destination. The 20,000 ton passenger liner was one of the firm's more recent acquisitions and controlled by a separate company, Lakonia Line, specially created for the purpose. (Her sister ship *Arkadia* was under the aegis of Arkadia Line). Registered with *Veritas*, the French equivalent of Lloyds of London and the American Bureau of Shipping, *Lakonia* was insured for over £1 million, half of it in the London market.

Her recent history was immaculate. The thirty years old former Dutch liner *Johan Van Oldenbarnebelt* had been taken over by Goulandris in Australia, sailed to Genoa for refitting (swimming pool, kindergarten, shops, sports and promenade decks, hospital, ballroom, everything a modern passenger liner required) and renamed *Lakonia*. She had a practised crew, mostly Greek with a sprinkling of Germans, and a Greek captain, Matheos Zarvis, an experienced master of the line.

Although the first radio signals reaching London did not paint a very dramatic picture of the situation, contact was immediately made with *Veritas*, the insurance company, and other authorities concerned with a shipping disaster. It appeared that the fire broke out in the ship's hairdressing salon and was feeding on the highly inflammable cosmetics on the shelves. Surely it could be put out with the fire equipment aboard which, as everything else in *Lakonia*, was new and up-to-date.

Signals arriving during the next few hours dashed the early optimism and unfolded the drama that was played out on the high seas. The six-hundred-odd passengers had been enjoying themselves at a fancy dress ball (theme: 'Dress as Tramps!') when the fire in the hairdressing salon was discovered. Captain Zarbis sounded the alarm but passengers were still joking and laughing as they left the big ballroom. What was happening on their ship was no laughing matter.

The fire would not yield to the extinguishers and the last of the revellers were only just leaving when the ballroom's parquet floor buckled from the heat below and started to break up. The situation was getting serious and passengers and crew soon realised the gravity of the situation. S.O.S. signals from the radio room reached half a dozen ships, the nearest some three hours sailing distance away. As people were making for the lifeboats, the fire was approaching the forward boats. Although they still kept their cool – 'As you might expect from the English', the captain said later – there was some pushing and shoving and the crew were later said to have been more anxious to save themselves than look after the passengers' safety.

The flames spread and generated terrific heat. When fifty oxygen bottles exploded near the second funnel the middle of the ship was engulfed in flames. One of the lifeboats plunged into the sea with fifty passengers aboard, another turned over as it hit the water. Passengers left behind on deck were faced with a petrifying dilemma. Burning or drowning – there did not seem to be another alternative. Getting frantic now, people jumped overboard hoping to keep afloat until rescue arrived. Behind them the flames were growing. Three hours elapsed before they saw the dim outline of a ship coming to their rescue.

London was following developments with bated breath. John Goulandris was told that the first ship on the scene was the British freighter *Montcalm*, followed by the Argentinian *Salta*. They moved forward gingerly – their information was that the *Lakonia* still had over five-hundred tons of fuel aboard which were liable to explode any minute. This seems to have worried the captains of the several other ships (*Stratheden, Charlesville, Independence, Rio Grande*) which steamed towards the burning vessel but kept at a safe distance.

Montcalm and *Salta* were picking up people from the boats and the sea as fast as they could when the *Lakonia's* captain issued a final desperate warning: '*Sauve qui peut!*' There were still about eighty passengers aboard, elderly people, mothers with babies in arms, the nervous and the timid. Fifty jumped overboard with the last members of the crew. The others seemed doomed. At long last the captain abandoned ship and took to a boat.

As dawn rose over the Atlantic, the fire-scarred hull of the *Lakonia* was a heart-rending sight. Two salvage tugs, the Norwegian *Herkules* and the Dutch *Clyde*, were nudging the wreck towards Gibraltar when the old vessel began to shudder, broke up and sank – 'a dreadful sight', according to the master of the *Clyde*. It was all over in three minutes and the *Lakonia*, or what was left of her, came to rest, 2,200 fathoms below the sea. The rescue ships delivered the shipwrecked passengers and crew to various ports; subject to adjustments, a head count summed up the full measure of the tragedy – ninety-six dead, thirty-one unaccounted for. Survivors: nine hundred and one.

The hue and cry that went up in the wake of her misfortune could be heard from shore to shore. The ugliest row developed in the United States where a feud among the *Rio Grande* crew erupted with wild accusations against the captain. Although he had picked up over seventy passengers, a lengthy indictment was drawn up against him criticising his rescue tactics – or lack of them. After examining the evidence, the owners cleared him of all guilt.

The captain of the *Independence* was also forced to defend himself against insinuations because he turned away from the scene of the disaster without joining in the rescue operations: 'There were so many ships', he countered, 'we were not needed.' The tragic individual stories, inevitable where so many lives were lost, sparked off controversy in Britain. Some passengers complained about the behaviour of the Greek crew and the apparent tardiness of rescue ships which kept at a safe distance from the burning *Lakonia* while German critics blamed the British ships for their 'cowardly approach to the disaster'.

Questions were asked in the House of Commons and there was sharp criticism of the *Lakonia's* owners in a thirteen-point memorandum which, in turn, was angrily repudiated by the Greek authorities. The Greeks themselves instituted an investigation which took two years to reach a conclusion: 'The fire in the hairdressing salon was a fortuitous event', the Greek report stated. Several deck officers were found guilty of negligence. But such was the prestige of the *Lakonia's* owners that the disputes, though they went on for three years, left no ill will behind. Goulandris ships sailed on serenely as the waves of the Atlantic washed away the memory of the tragedy.

The eighteenth floor of Lee House, a modern office block in a small, secluded square in the City of London, is occupied by the firm of N. J. Goulandris. The stream-lined shipping office is supervised with military efficiency by one of the directors, – G. Bisbas, whose bearing and manner betrays his background of twelve years service with the Greek army.

However difficult to reconcile with the clockwork proceedings of the smoothly-run organisation, N. J. Goulandris is the child of a revolution, rare in the tightly-knit Greek shipping families. The new firm came about as the result of a breakaway from Goulandris Bros. which united old Petros' sons

Basil, Nicholas and Leonidas and their own off-spring under one umbrella.

All was well until 1952 when, impatient with the old boys' methods and outlook, the sons of Nicholas turned their backs on the firm and set themselves up in business on their own. Though officially described as 'a friendly parting of the ways', the revolt earned the chief instigator, John N. (Hirohito) Goulandris the new nickname of Nasser – Colonel Nasser's revolution against King Farouk's regime was making the headlines at the time. Twin brothers Leonidas N. and Alexander N. Goulandris joined John in the new venture.

The three brothers are typical of the new generation of Greek shipowners. In Andros, where he was born in 1924, John N. grew up to a boyhood vastly different from that of the traditional Greek captains. While they went to sea in their early teens in ramshackle boats subsisting on meagre rations and working their fingers to the bone, John's first encounters with the sea were in sleek sailing yachts which he learned to master with consummate skill. From matching his skill against the sea, he went on to fight the enemies of Greece. He was still in school in Athens when he joined the resistance against the Germans who occupied the country. After the war he studied law and economics at Lausanne, Switzerland, before going on to the United States to learn the rudiments of the shipping business.

The next stop was London where he joined the family firm, Goulandris Bros. which owned some thirty ships, among them several Liberty vessels and the passenger liners *Nea Ellas* (later renamed *New York*), *Campera* and *Columbia*. Restless, ambitious and a little bored with the routine of the sedate shipping office, John put much of his surplus energy into sailing and steered a succession of fine boats to victory. *Miss Enfield*, the best known of his boats, once raced – for the benefit of television – at speeds of up to eighty miles through a twenty foot gap in the rocks off the Isle of Wight.

Attuned to such speed he could not reconcile himself to Goulandris Bros'. slow-motion operations. The elderly gentlemen of the family were wedded to the old tradition, their sons joining the business as they came of age, made it a crowded organisation. After barely two years, John N. wanted out. He talked it over with the senior partners who were shocked by the revolutionary ideas of the imaginative newcomer. Hirohito staged his revolution, taking his and his brother's share of the assets – five of the thirty-two Goulandris Bros'. vessels – with him into his own company, N. J. Goulandris. Uncle Leonidas' sons at the same time took the passenger ships into their own new firm, Ormos.

Nothing is more complicated than to break up an old Greek shipping empire. Each member of the family owns a share in the enterprise of his father, uncles, brothers, cousins. The separation of interests left 'Hirohito-Nasser' and his brothers also in control of four Liberty vessels. *Ev Anthia*, *I. P. Goulandris*, *Chryssie* and *Petros* which Goulandris Bros. acquired from the first batch of Liberty ships and passed on to Orion, now landed in the safe harbour of N. J. Goulandris. Altogether, the firm started with a splendid little fleet to build on.

There was plenty of capital in the kitty and John N. organised his life in the manner to which Greek shipping millionaires are accustomed. He bought a town house in Chelsea and one of the finest stately homes of England, Ashdown House, in Ashdown Park, Berkshire, scene of the historical battle in which King Ethelred of Wessex and his brother, Alfred the Great, defeated the Danes in A.D. 871. The house was completely modernised except for the original staircase which remains as it was when it was built for the first Earl of Craven. With it went a farm at Lambourne.

His yacht *Triaina* is one of the finest afloat. She is based on Vouliagmene, next door to brother Alexander's 370 ton yacht *Anemos*, which is no mean ship either. Alexander has made *Anemos* his home where he lives with his wife Marietta, née Nomikos, and their three girls but also has a London house in Eaton Square.

John N. who has everything except a wife is active in many spheres outside his shipping firm. He owns Enfield Automotive which builds electric cars and Enfield Diesel Motors – it is the

Enfield connection to which his speedboat owes its name. Another of his ventures is a small shipyard at Cowes which he regards largely as a hobby without neglecting its commercial potentialities. Production of fibreglass speedboats may soon make it viable.

His approach to N. J. Goulandris is as energetic. Soon after the company's inception, he started a major shipbuilding programme by placing orders in Japanese yards from which his new tankers and dry cargo vessels began to issue in 1956. The first, a 35,000 ton tanker, was named *Alexandra I* after his little niece – the daughter of his sister Anne whose second husband is Greek actor Dimitri Horn ('No party is complete without them,' gushed New York society columnist Suzy). Next, in quick succession, came two 17,500 ton dry cargo vessels, *Granada* and *Aragon*, and a 35,000 tonner, *Castella*. Three more dry cargo vessels, 16,000 tons each, were named after English counties – *Derby*, *Cornwall* and *Devon*.

John had not done yet. As all Greek shipowners do sooner or later, he returned to his origins in the Aegean sea – and thereby hangs the story of the great Greek revival as a base for shipowners who went out to make their own way in *xenitia*. The new development can be traced back to the six-day war between Israel and the Arabs when international enterprises with major Middle East branches began to look for safer bases. As some of them transferred their offices to Greece, the Greek Government, *pour encourager les autres*, introduced new legislation and offered tax concessions which made it extremely attractive for foreigners to establish headquarters in Greece. The Colonels turned the country into a new haven for shipowners offering conditions comparable to the Central American flag of convenience countries.

Though not specifically designed for the shipping industry and applying over a wide range of industry, Greek shipowners in *xenitia* promptly availed themselves of the new facilities, the biggest operators heading the rush back to their native land where they registered their ships under the Greek flag of convenience. Greek registered tonnage increased by leaps and bounds, shipping offices sprouted all over Piraeus, and the growing volume of shipping business offered employment and new opportunities. Under the new measures owners operating from Greece were exempted from the obligation to declare their foreign incomes – exactly the reverse of American legislation which drove the New York Greeks in headlong flight from the United States.

For John Goulandris, as for many of his fellow shipowners, this was the moment to take the plunge. He returned to Greece but not to his native Andros. After a thorough investigation and protracted negotiations he acquired the historic Neorion Shipyard on Siros, cradle of the earliest Greek trading ships. Originally built by Captain Nicholas Rethymnis as a repair yard, John Goulandris decided to renovate and expand Neorion with an investment of some fifteen million dollars.

Plans for a new graving dock at Pedall involved deepening of the harbour to take vessels of 100,000 tons, and orders went out for new automatic equipment, machinery and cranes. Representatives of European heavy industry – Krupp of Essen among them – converged on Siros in search of contracts. They ended up – in prison! No, not in the Colonels' dungeons but in the ancient prison of Lazaretta which N. J. Goulandris rebuilt and refurbished as their headquarters on Siros. John was already looking further ahead and promised to build training schools for marine engineers and naval architects on the island.

While John established himself on the island of Siros, the family's native island of Andros also made an impact. Almost at the same time as work began on the new installations on Siros, the bulky but graceful 230,000 ton *Andros Orion* joined the Orion fleet whose ships keep the name of Andros alive and started to earn her cost of around twenty million dollars and, in the inexorable way of Greek shipping, breed more of her kind.

In the final quarter of 1971, millions of tons were added to the Greek-owned merchant fleet. Onassis was taking delivery of four super-tankers, amounting to nearly a million tons –

Olympic Anthem, 228,000 tons (from a French yard); *Olympic Alliance*, *Olympic Ambition* and *Olympic Archer*, each 216,000 tons and all three built in Japan.

Goulandris interests were about to match this gigantic array of tankers ton for ton.

XII

THE HEIRS OF ODYSSEUS

CHURCH bells ringing, salutes and loud bangs splitting the air over Ithaca. The small, rocky Ionian island far off the beaten tourist track in festive garb. People flocking to the harbour to watch the white, tall, elegant *Christina* edging closer. Stepping ashore with Greta Garbo on his arm, Aristotle Onassis looked bewildered: 'What's the matter?' he asked. 'Is it an earthquake? A fire?'

'Not at all' came the answer from the island's dignitaries there to welcome the illustrious visitors: 'This is in your honour!'

Greta Garbo was not the only celebrity Onassis took to the island of his dreams. Ithaca was a port of call when he went cruising with Winston Churchill, and again in October 1963, when he sailed with President Kennedy's wife who was recuperating after a miscarriage (a month before the President's tragic death). It was in Ithaca – Onassis acting as a solicitous and erudite guide – that he formed his close friendship with Jackie Kennedy which ripened into marriage five years later.

Onassis' early career in shipping, his very beginnings were bound up with Ithaca which Homer described as 'a precipitous isle, unfit for horses, good for goats'. It became, to use Onassis' own words, 'a base for the human element' of his shipping operations. Most of the sailors who manned his ships, many of the captains he engaged as masters came from Ithaca, the island of Odysseus with whom he feels such a strong affinity and with whom he shares the smell of the sea, the adventurous, peripatetic life, the unorthodox outlook unfettered by the stereotype routine of lesser men, and perhaps even, it has often occurred to me, the favour of the gods.

In his homes in Paris and Athens and on *Christina* he keeps a voluminous library devoted to Homeriana and to Odysseus

Minos Colocotronis and the
Santa Maja

ABOVE E. M. J. Colocotronis and Minos
Colocotronis. RIGHT Antony Giorgiadis and
Alex Giorgiadis, partners of Colocotronis.

Two famous Oinoussians: John Hadjipateras (left), shipowner, publisher, writer, scion of the Pateras-Hadjipateras clan, and Marcos Lemos, airman and stud-owner, with the author

– his prize exhibit is an imposing volume entitled *Ulysse-Homere, ou Du Veritable Auteur de l'Iliade et de l'Odyssee*, by Constantine Koliades, Professor of the Ionian University, dating from 1829. He has studied the Trojan War and the history of the legendary King of Ithaca whose twelve men-of-war joined the Greek armada when, 3,182 years ago, it set out for Troy to recover Queen Helena of Sparta who had been abducted by Paris, the play-boy prince. They destroyed Troy in the war which lasted ten years but Odysseus travelled on for another decade.

Unlike Odysseus, Onassis has returned to the island again and again and the conversations between him and his shipping associates sometimes recall the famous 'Debate in Ithaca' before Odysseus' son Telemachus sailed in seach of his father. Onassis still visits the famous Monastery of Kethara perched high on Mount Niritos: 'I have adopted the island' he is fond of saying, sometimes correcting himself: 'Maybe Ithaca has adopted me'. Ithaca reciprocated his affection and has made him an honorary citizen.

Onassis was desolate when an earthquake played havoc with the island in 1953, The tragedy gave birth to his ambition to have an island of his own as near as possible to the kingdom of Odysseus. When tiny Skorpios island ten miles north of Ithaca, came on the market, he snatched it up and turned it into his private paradise.

What the people of Ithaca and the other six Ionian islands share with the descendants of Smyrna (like Onassis), is an association with an alien culture. Smyrna's eastern culture was different from the Greek heritage; Ionian architecture, outlook and customs, bear the hallmark of four centuries (1386-1797) of Venetian domination. Though Ionian Greeks used to complain bitterly that Venice treated them harsher than the Ottoman Empire they have long changed their tune, and now boast about their Venetian background which makes them feel superior to their Aegean compatriots. The long spell of British rule which followed the Venetian period also left a mark.

The old port of Ithaca is enclosed by a semi-circle formed by two streets which are named after two of the island's leading shipping personalities, George Dracoulis Street and Captain Gratsos Street. The two names are at the root of Onassis' affection for the island which dated back to 1923 when he first arrived in Buenos Aires, a poor refugee from Smyrna with only a few dollars in his pocket.

Three years later, he had made his first million from tobacco deals and met Costa Gratsos, son of the sea captain from Ithaca from whom the harbour street takes its name. An apprentice seaman on a Dracoulis ship, young Gratsos enjoyed the hectic social life of Buenos Aires and the company of prosperous Argentinian and exile Greeks with whom Onassis associated. The two became close friends – without Gratsos Onassis might never have discovered his love for Ithaca.

Costa Gratsos is often described as the genius whose know-how and acumen helped to raise Onassis to his eminence in shipping. Gratsos himself, now Vice-President of Victory Carriers, the American shipping corporation controlled by the Onassis Trust, dismisses the suggestion: 'It is not true,' he said emphatically, when I discussed the old times with him. 'I knew a great deal about ships and advised Onassis but it was his financial genius that carried him to the top'.

Costa Gratsos is steeped in shipping which is Ithaca's heritage since Odysseus. What he communicated to the young land-lubber from Asia Minor – apart from the love of Ithaca – was the feel of ships of which Onassis knew little more than he had seen from the heights of Smyrna when watching them on their way towards the high seas. They talked about the island's shipping history and the statistics which every son of Ithaca has at his fingertips.

According to English records quoted by Nicos S. Vlassopulos from Ithaca (not surprisingly a Vlassopulos is a director of the Onassis organisation), forty per cent of Ithaca's male population, men and boys, were working in ships at the beginning of the nineteenth century when seventeen vessels, a total of 1,480 tons, were registered in Ithaca. Fifteen other Ithaca-owned ships (1,890 tons) sailed under the Russian 'flag of convenience' and islanders also controlled thirty smaller craft and ninety boats. By the time Britain restored the Ionian islands to Greece in 1864 (as a gesture to the Danish prince who was crowned King George I of Greece) Ithaca's fleet had grown to a grand total of 5,000 tons.

Apart from the sea, the island did not offer its adventurous sons much of a living. John Theophilatos, who became the king of Ithaca's shipping, was the first of many to seek his fortune in *xenitia*, went to Rumania and settled in Galati where his brothers joined him. Cousin Otton Stathatos was not far behind, Vlassopulos, Dracoulis and Callinicos (another name in the Onassis hierachy), soon followed suit.

All were inter-related and worked together exporting grain and importing coal and made a great deal of money. They discovered the opportunities of the Danube as a trade route and bought ships to carry their merchandise. Theophilatos acquired his first ship in May 1873 and named her *Ithaca*. His second, bought in 1877, was the 978 tons *Odysseus*.

The Danube ports of Galati and Braila became centres of Ionian shipping and by 1890 the register of the Greek Consulate in Braila listed four hundred and sixty large river barges, seventy-five flat-bottomed lighters and forty-four tug ice-breakers, a total of 83,000 tons, of which almost three-quarters belonged to the wealthy merchants-turned-shipowners from Ithaca. They soon went over to steam, built and operated grain elevators introducing considerable technical improvements. Their techniques were adopted in many parts of the world. John Theophilatos' son Dimitri introduced the technique of mechanical discharge of grain to Rotterdam whose official history gratefully acknowledges his contribution.

Islanders who had no ships of their own worked as captains, pilots, agents and ship chandlers. In winter when the Danube was icebound they returned home to court, marry, make love and produce children. In those long, gloomy winter months when the placid Ionian sea around them was whipped by storms they talked of ships and ships and ships, of Theophilatos buying yet another vessel, of the growing Vlassopulos fleet and Stathatos investing in more and bigger vessels.

At the end of the nineteenth century Ithaca boasted an indigenous tonnage of 28,000 tons. Business – particularly the business of Theophilatos and Stathatos – expanded so fast that they set up agencies in Antwerp, Rotterdam, Cardiff and, eventually, London. In the first decade of the new century, Dracoulis and Gratsos were also heading for London – Gratsos to buy ships and the Dracoulis family to settle in the centre of world shipping.

There were setbacks, Vlassopulos lost two of his three ships, both uninsured. The *Andriana Stathatos*, named after the owner's wife, went down with all hands, every one of them from Ithaca. Another ship owned jointly by a captain and an engineer from Ithaca foundered on her maiden voyage and the whole crew was lost. Year after year, the island mourned its sons whose grave was the sea.

Still, salt water was the life blood of Ithaca. Inspired by western ideas, the islanders introduced democracy into shipping establishing a public company to which most of the population subscribed. In 1902, the Ithaca consortium bought its first ship, a vessel of 2,849 tons, which did so well that a second, larger one, was added four years later, and eventually five more, totalling 17,000 tons, all built in England. The handsome profits were shared out enabling many small shareholders to buy ships of their own.

As Ithaca shipping prospered, the name of Theophilatos, engraved on the cradle of the island's seafaring exploits, was fading from the scene. An ardent Greek patriot, the head of the firm lost interest in shipping and turned to politics, holding meetings and pleading the Greek cause. As President of the Ellenismos Club, he addressed the members at a ceremonial occasion and raised his glass of Champagne for a toast to the future of a united Greece. It was his last gesture to his beloved country. With the glass in his hand, he collapsed and died. His three sons were as patriotic as their father. They sold the ships, closed up shop and joined Venizelos in his fight for the union of Greece.

A colourful personality with a sparkling intellect who looks less than fifty but was fast approaching seventy when I talked to him in New York, Costa Gratsos added the flavour of his family history to the story of Ithaca. Starting his working day at seven-thirty a.m. he is at his desk in the Onassis Victory Carriers office in New York's Fifth Avenue (now temporarily at other premises while building is in progress) long before the staff arrives. His telephone rings incessantly as he keeps in touch with business associates and friends all over the world. Most of them are Greeks.

That morning newspapers carried reports of a May Day revolution in Panama where many Onassis ships are registered. They said that a Labour Government had taken over. Gratsos called his friend, Panama's President Don Demetrio Laka on the telephone, but the President, who is of Greek origin, soon reassured him: 'They've all been locked up. They are all in prison!'

Costa Gratsos smiled contentedly. Another threat to Greek shipping was averted. His mind was free to roam over the past which Greeks never tire of recounting. His origin is firmly rooted among Ithaca's premier families – many Ionians marry women from foreign parts and are as proud of them as they are contemptuous of the near-incestuous inter-marriages so frequent in the Aegean islands. Grandmother Calliope was a sister of John Theophilatos and married to a Dracoulis. Grandfather Dimitrios Gratsos, an artist with no shipping background, owned olive groves and oil presses and traded in timber which he imported from Dalmatia. The youngest of his twelve children, George Gratsos, reverted to shipping, worked for Stathatos and became a captain. He saved, built a house and, in 1901 at the age of thirty, took Polyxene Dracoulis as a bride. As was the custom in Ithaca, wedding festivities went on for three days of drinking and dancing and merry-making.

After a brief honeymoon George Gratsos went back to sea

and his wife did not see him again until he brought his ship home in summer. The following year their first boy was born. Costa was seven days old when he first 'went to sea' and is proud of it. His three brothers, Alchimos, Dimitri and Panos who came along in quick succession, found their sea-legs as early. 'Captain George Gratsos', Costa says of his father, 'was ambitious and full of ideas!' It was at his suggestion that brother-in-law Constantine Dracoulis, whose tugs and river barges operated in Rumania, bought his first steamship in the year Costa was born. Not many years later the Gratsos family had outgrown their native island and moved to Athens.

The Greek islanders' cult of naming the first-born sons after their fathers is so well-established, it almost comes as a shock when a family loses one of its traditional names. This is what happened to a forefather of the cultivated and charming gentleman who lives at 7, Grosvenor Square in one of the £100,000 apartments with the splendour of a palace (marble columns and all), and is known as George Dracoulis. That should not be his name. Not George! The name of George is a break with tradition in a family whose first recorded ancestor was Jacobus Dracoulis (b. 1690).

Old Jacobus' name should have turned up in every other generation but there has been no Jacobus since 1864 when a baby boy was born into the family with every right to his ancestor's first name. This, you may remember, was the year King George I ascended the throne, and in his honour parents named their boys born at this auspicious time after the King. Instead of Jacobus, the new-born Dracoulis became George, and the name has come down to George Dracoulis of Grosvenor Square.

In the home of the contemporary George Dracoulis, Ithaca's British connection is much in evidence. One painting depicts an imposing, splendidly-gowned ancestor, Judge Eustace Dracoulis (1814-1874) who represented Queen Victoria as Governor of Ithaca. In the Greek *Who's Who* successive Dracoulis occupy fourteen pages and George's library with the leather-bound classics, art books and modern literature (Sartre strongly represented) contains a volume of the family history which is so involved that George has to consult it before pronouncing on the family tree.

The long line of Constantines begins with the one born in 1735, but soon comes down to Constantine Dracoulis who married Calliope Theophilatos and had seven children, four girls (the youngest became Captain Gratsos' wife) and three boys, the 1864 George Dracoulis and his two brothers, Pericles and Hector. All four after completing their education in Ithaca, Cephalonia and Athens joined the Theophilatos shipping business, went to Russia and Rumania, worked hard and prospered. Worked and prayed. The three brothers never missed mass on Sunday and Pericles sonorous voice was a popular asset to the choir.

The acute business sense of the elder George Dracoulis is part of the modern story of Ithaca. When he travelled to England to buy this third steamship, the 6,400 ton *Telemachus*, which was built to his specifications, he handed over the price of £40,000 in cash, soon added three more ships (*Laertes*, *Polyktor* and *Niritos*) to his fleet, all cash on the nail.

Ships were built quickly in these days. The market was buoyant, trading was easy. Captain George Gratsos supervised the building of the Dracoulis ships in England, then sent them on their voyages taking grain from the Danube to Marseilles, Rotterdam and Newcastle, and coal from England to Italy and Rumania. Gravitating towards the western shipping centres, the Dracoulis brothers blazed the trail to London where they established their shipping agency, G. K. Dracoulis Brothers, ten years before Kulukundis of Kasos arrived on the scene. Captain George Gratsos was made a full partner of the firm, with headquarters in Athens.

George Dracoulis travelled the world and became a pioneer of the luxury hotel habit which is still characteristic of Greek shipowners. His brother Pericles was less peripatetic and made his home in England. He and his wife Olga, whose people were landowners in Ithaca, settled in North London and their house remained in the family for many decades. Hector, the youngest brother, married to the former Calliope Korvissian, a winegrower's daughter, also came to live in London.

Distance did not separate the brothers from the island of their birth. They put up funds to install electricity in their native village of Perachoria, financed the building of roads and maintained the old Georgian-style family mansion, the birthplace of John Metaxas who became Prime Minister of Greece in 1936. (After being destroyed in the earthquake of 1953, the house was lovingly restored.)

From London where their agency went from strength to strength, the Dracoulis brothers followed the stormy lives of their cousins who had sold their ships and invested in real estate. Dimitri Theophilatos joined the Greek army to fight in the Balkan wars and, when this came to an end and World War One broke out, picked another fight. For him the issue was not one of the Western Allies versus the Central Powers. Greece was his only concern.

Outraged when the British forced King Constantine I of Greece to abdicate because being married to the Kaiser's sister Sophie, he favoured the Germans, Dimitri Theophilatos declared war on the British Empire. With a fine feeling for Greek mythology, he aimed his attack at the Achilles heel of his mighty foe (Achilles was said to be invulnerable except for a spot on his heel), went to the United States and came out in support of Britain's implacable Irish enemy Eamonn de Valera whose campaign against the British he financed.

The Irish prevailed but Dimitri Theophilatos went broke. He moved to Rotterdam, scene of his early technical triumphs, and set himself up as a shipbroker. A decade and a half later he went to Spain to join the Republicans against France, another lost cause. A forgotten man, he died in the late forties. Since neither he nor his brothers were married this was the end of the line.

Demetrios Stathatos, the last of Ithaca's other pioneering family, also went out of shipping. Married to an English woman, he had a daughter but no son and heir, sold his ships and retired to Nice where he lives with his memories – not that his part is forgotten by Greek shipping men who hold him in great esteem.

At the outbreak of the first world war twenty-six ships, nearly 50,000 tons, were registered in Ithaca. Dracoulis and Gratsos sold the *Odysseus* and replaced her with a ship of the same name. She was lost in the Atlantic early in the war, her sister ship *Niritos* suffered the same fate and their third ship. *Laertes*, was torpedoed in the Mediterranean. Altogether eleven of Ithaca's ships perished in the war but the crews were saved. The men of Ithaca had to start again from scratch – with only the insurance money to sustain them. Dracoulis dabbled in other industries, sold his share in a bank in Piraeus to the Commercial Bank of Greece, and acquired a brewery in Athens, which still belongs to the family.

The four Gratsos brothers, Costa, Dimitri, Alchimos and Panos were separated. Dimitri went into shipping in the United States, Alchimos who acquired a Ph.D. (chemistry) continued his studies in Athens, is the only one who stayed in Greece to look after the family interests including the brewery. Panos went into business on his own and settled in London. Costa was inevitably drawn into the Onassis orbit.

Since the twenties, the two men frequently travelled in harness. Costa Gratsos introduced Onassis to Uncle Pericles who was the first broker to buy ships for Onassis in London. Ari and Costa did not allow business to interfere with pleasure. Their nightly extravaganzas shocked Pericles but left him with a healthy regard for Onassis' inexhaustible energy. Onassis was also adept at choosing useful aides, like George Callinicos, Dracoulis' marine superintendent who joined him as consulting engineer, the beginning of a long association.

In the early thirties ship prices were low and Costa Gratsos urged Onassis to buy. He gave the same advice to his brothers: 'They did not believe me,' he sighs. 'That's why we are not as big as we might have been.' He wrote about shipping in *Naftika Chronika* and travelled a great deal. Though he pursued his own interests he crossed the path of Onassis again and

again. If Onassis needed support for his unorthodox faith in
bigger and bigger tankers, Costa Gratsos gave it in no uncertain terms.

'I promoted large vessels as firmly as I could,' he told me.
'Tankers, bulk carriers – ships that could carry twice the cargo
with a crew not bigger than needed for ships of half the size.
It was a matter of port facilities. Rotterdam and Amsterdam
for instance, were quite capable of taking larger vessels.' The
first to follow Costa's lead was not Onassis, not even a shipowner but – a stamp collector by the name of Frixos Papachristiris.

'One night in Montreal, in a bar – where else?' Gratsos
said. 'I explained the advantage of big ships and Frixos put
up 1.2 million dollars to build a 20,000 ton vessel – giants of
the sea in these days. Onassis was not far behind. Defying
'expert opinion' and obstruction from sceptical ship-builders,
he ordered bigger and bigger tankers.

For ever exploring new avenues, or rather sea lanes, Costa
Gratsos was intrigued by the rich potentialities of the Far
East trade and went out in the family's good ship *Kastor* to
investigate. For two years (1935-1937) he roamed the seas
from the River Plate to the Pacific, studied the timber and
copra trade in British Columbia and visited China, Japan,
the Philippines: '*Kastor* mapped out the route all the Greeks
followed!'

Ithaca shipping was still expanding – in tonnage rather than
ships – and at the outbreak of war in 1939, the island's register
listed twenty-five vessels with a total of nearly 100,000 tons.
In the United States, Costa Gratsos was appointed a maritime
consul of the Greek Government in exile – his most important
job was to look after some four hundred Greek sailors stranded
on the wrong side of the Atlantic. Aristotle Onassis was living
in Los Angeles and there was constant to-ing and fro-ing from
coast to coast, the two friends getting together as often as
possible.

They engaged in all sorts of enterprises including Onassis'
first venture into whaling off the coast of California, an hilarious

experience. With Costa's help, Onassis discovered an old Californian whaling station under the name of *Eureka*. Eureka! Costa examined the proposition which required only a little capital, no more than 15,000 dollars. The two whaling novices chartered a couple of old, delapidated tug boats, engaged a Swedish gunner and one other aide: 'He was always drunk', Gratsos recalled. For a suitable reward U.S. coastguards helped to spot shoals of whales from their balloons.

The operation was neither spectacular nor unprofitable. The two-boat fleet managed to kill some thirty to forty whales (Gratsos: 'Big Deal!'), enough to start an oil production. The partners switched to selling whale meat to mink farms ('minks are mad about it') and finally sold the whole outfit to the Borden Company which was producing 'Vitamin A' from shark livers and was looking for whale livers to supplement the supply.

While Alchimos Gratsos joined the Greek army in Athens and fought in Albania, the Gratsos ships *Triton* (7,500 tons) and *Kastor* (10,500 tons) were recruited for war service with the allies. For *Triton* is was a short career – she was sunk in the English Channel in 1939. *Kastor* sailed on until 1942 when an Italian submarine caught up with her near Trinidad and sent her to the bottom of the sea. One consolation – the crews, mostly from Ithaca, were saved. When the war was over, Ithaca mourned fourteen of its twenty-five ships.

In New York, in the meantime, Costa Gratsos quickly grasped the significance of the American offer of Liberty ships for the Greeks and simply could not understand why some of his compatriots dithered over the transaction. Several of them were persuaded by him – he literally talked them into taking the ships and making their fortune.

It was not a one-way affair. With civil war raging in Greece, not everybody was keen to see the hotly disputed Liberty vessels go to a country in turmoil. At the same time, the British and Norwegians were worried lest a big allocation to the Greeks cut down their own share. Washington hesitated on the brink of a final decision and there was a risk that the ingenious scheme, initiated by Manuel Kulukundis, might collapse. The arguments were not settled when the date for the final Greek application was already at hand.

Costa Gratsos decided to tip the scales. In the nick of time he remembered his friend Ed Pauley whom he first knew as a struggling politician in the thirties and helped with valuable contacts: 'If ever you need help', Costas recalled the grateful Ed telling him, 'I shall be glad to do everything in my power.' Now Ed Pauley was President Truman's closest adviser and a powerful man in Washington.

On the critical evening, Gratsos was at the Greek Embassy with Ambassador Diamandopoulos who was afraid that the Greek owners might miss the boat – the Liberty ships. Gratsos called Pauley who sent a White House car to collect him: 'We settled the matter in a short conference,' Gratsos said. 'By one p.m. everything was fixed!' Of the Liberty ships distributed among Greek owners, ten went to Ithaca, four of them to Gratsos Bros. They named the first *G. D. Gratsos*, after their father, and the others *Oros Athos* (after the mountain on Ithaca), *Triton* and *Kastor* after the ships they had lost.

When Costa Gratsos took up the cudgels on behalf of Onassis, he was less successful. Not having been a Greek flag operator and, what's more, not having lost a ship in the war, Onassis did not qualify for an allocation. He took it hard, as we have seen from the aggressive round robin he circulated and for which Gratsos generously accepted the blame – 'It was all really a joke,' he told me.

Only a man as persuasive and charming as he could hope to overcome the ill-feeling the affair caused. His admiration for Manuel Kulukundis was, and still is, unstinted: 'Thanks to him', he said, 'many Greeks prospered, including Costa Lemos.' Brushing aside the smouldering animosities, he brought together a group of men who were by no means natural allies, and actually managed to get Onassis, Niarchos and Kulukundis to join him in a shipping enterprise, the Pacific-Mediterranean Line, to ply between the West Coast of America, Cuba (not as yet Castro's) and the Mediterranean, but the venture did not live long.

For Alchimos Gratsos the lure of shipping proved too strong. While Costa was operating on the other side of the Atlantic, he started his own firm in Athens, George Gratsos Limited which operates eight tramp ships in world-wide trade. Though not a seaman, he was elected Chairman of the Greek Chamber of Shipping and Vice President of the Union of Greek Ship-owners. His two sons are following in the family tradition – George who was born in 1942 (Alchimos: 'The year the *Kastor* was sunk') graduated from the Massachusetts Institute of Technology and is a naval architect; and Costa junior (born 1945) an economics graduate of the University of Geneva, is a shipbroker.

The elder Costa Gratsos continued in the wake of Onassis. Forever anxious not to detract from the glory of his friend and chief ('The most wonderful man in the world, remarkable, more than a brother to me'), he is over-modest when talking about his past in the Onassis operations but some of his feats cannot be overlooked.

Perhaps his most spectacular success if associated with Onassis' second and big-time whaling operation in the nine-teen-fifties when the Onassis whaling fleet made a good deal of money but also involved the owner in one nerve-testing international incident after another – it was bombarded by the Peruvian Air Force and viciously attacked by Norwegian competitors. Anticipating a decline in the market as operating costs went up and crews wanted higher wages, Onassis, by 1955, decided it was a good time to sell.

Costas Gratsos happened to be in Tokyo on business of his own when he received a call from Onassis: 'If you can dispose of the whaling fleet – do it!' From his suite at the *Imperial Hotel*, he put out feelers – he had been in at the beginning of the whaling adventure, now he was going to bring it to an end. Onassis wanted something like six million dollars for the factory ship and fifteen catchers, perhaps a little more. Seeing an opportunity to please his friend, Gratsos set out to find the right buyer. It took him nine months of 'joyful battle for big stakes' to get a respectable offer. After some hard bargaining he made a deal with the *Whaling Company Kyokuyo Hogei Kaisha* which only needed the seal of approval from Onassis.

Awaiting the dawn of the European working day at the Gimbasha (The Silver Horse) night-club, Gratsos put through a call to Onassis at Monte Carlo. It was 4 a.m. Tokyo time when Onassis came on the line: 'We've got a deal!' Gratsos shouted. Obviously waiting to hear the most important thing, the price, Onassis said nothing: 'I sold for 8.5 million dollars,' Gratsos said. After another pause, Onassis asked slowly: 'Where are you?' 'At the *Gimbasha*' Gratsos replied. 'You're drunk' Onassis retorted, then burst out laughing. Costa Gratsos had never been more sober. He had brought off a big coup.

In recent years Costa Gratsos has given most of his time to his work as Vice-President of Victory Carriers and become associated with some of the biggest operations of this Onassis Trust Corporation which increased in importance when the Kennedy administration took over in 1960 and put the squeeze on foreign interests in the United States. The New York Greeks were the principal victims of the new legislation which required all non-American enterprises to declare their assets and income in foreign countries and pay American taxes.

With their international interests and 'flag of convenience' fleets, the Greeks were not anxious to shoulder these new obligations. The biggest and most active operators reduced their American establishments to a minimum, packed their bags and returned to Europe. The Kennedy Legislation – dirty words in the Greek shipping vocabulary – put an end to the New York Greeks as a closely-knit, homogenous shipping group.

The shipping corporations of the Onassis Trust, specifically created as American enterprises in the names of Onassis' American-born children, were not subject to these trouble-some and costly ordinances and enjoyed the privileges of indigenous organisations. The trust ships were eligible to carry war supplies, as foreign-owned vessels were not. On the other hand, they were obliged to pay American taxes which put them at a disadvantage against flag-of-convenience owners who were not liable to American taxation.

As Vice-President of Victory Carriers, Costa Gratsos had the added advantage of being an American citizen at the head of an American corporation. American interests were close to his heart. In the mid-sixties, Victory Carriers were planning to build a 100,000 ton tanker but was told that the U.S. Navy for logistic reasons would prefer two ships of 47,000 tons each instead. Onassis readily agreed but left it to Gratsos to pacify the builders at Bethlehem Steel's Sparrow Point Yard, who were none too pleased about the last-minute switch which involved intricate re-planning.

On another occasion, Gratsos and Captain Alfred H. Riggs, another Victory Carriers's executive, were called to Washington to meet Admiral Donaho, commander of Military Transportation who told a gathering of shipowners that the United States was looking to the industry to keep prices down. Onassis complied and Victory Carriers was among the first shipping organisations to tender its ships to the Navy without capitalising on the shortage of tonnage which was forcing prices up.

Costa's brother Dimitri joined the New York branch of the Vergottis shipping interests (a name not popular with Onassis as will presently emerge), but the 'Brothers Karamasov', as the trade calls the Gratsos brothers, remained as closely united as any Greek shipping family. Though Costa spends many vacations at his house in Miami, in summer the brothers often congregate in Ithaca where they can be seen strolling along the street which bears their father's name and towards the house Captain George Gratsos built at the beginning of the century. They may have become part of the big world of New York, London and Athens but they are still at home in Ithaca.

The Dracoulis family never recaptured the shipping glories of yore. Old George did not long survive the war. Pericles stayed in London and sent his son Constantine to Radley College, a well-known English public school. The young man joined the Royal Air Force in the last war and was killed in action – it is still not clear whether he lost his life on a secret mission in enemy-occupied Greece or was shot down by the Luftwaffe.

Pericles died in 1946. His widow, Olga, spent the rest of her life in England and when she died twenty-four years after her husband, her bequests reflected the family's loyalties, equally divided between Ithaca and Britain. She left £50,000 to *Enosis Ithakision*, an organisation devoted to development of her native island. Another bequest went to the Dracoulis Memorial Fund which finances exchange visits of Greek and English children. In memory of her son, the R.A.F. Benevolent Fund and Radley figured prominently in the will.

Two of Hector Dracoulis' sons, Constantine (borne 1916) and George (1923) spent the war in Greece but returned to London as soon as it was over. They became popular figures in racing circles and Constantine's sky-blue and scarlet colours were carried to many triumphs but luck was not always with him. He sold his horse, *Primera*, only to see it win a £10,000 race for its new owner a few days later. In 1961 he sold his racing interests.

Constantine earned a reputation as a generous, not to say extravagant host. Two dozen tables at one of his parties were covered with tablecloths said to have cost £400 each. George was never far behind. His pre-wedding stag party at the *Mirabelle* Restaurant was a lavish affair and his wedding reception at *Claridge's* the highlight of the 1958 London season. His bride was the blonde, vivacious Mitsa Pateras who, as her name indicates, hails from Oinoussai and is a cousin of Maro Hadjipateras.

Constantine and George carried on the family brokerage but things did not go well for them. In 1963 they closed down the old firm. The winding up of the highly respected business after over fifty years of existence came as a shock to the City of London but did not cramp the style of the brothers, who are still wealthy by any standards.

Altogether, Ithaca, the romantic ancient island of their birth from which Odysseus went forth to fight the most celebrated war in history has not matched the shipping triumphs of lesser and less attractive rocks in the emerald waters around Greece.

XIII

HOME IS THE SAILOR

THE squat, unending tanker heaved away from London
Docks. 40,000 tons of ship ploughed through the English
Channel into the Atlantic, turned south and entered the
Mediterranean at Gibraltar continuing its voyage along the
coast of North Africa and passing Sicily and Malta before
turning north towards the Ionian Sea. On the hull gleamed
her name – *Cephalonia*.

No tanker ever sailed on a sadder mission. On that twelve-
day trip in the summer of 1968, the *Cephalonia's* holds were
empty. Except for its own fuel, there was not a drop of oil
aboard. The only cargo she carried towards the Greek island
after which it was named, was the coffin of one of Cephalonia's
sons. Having been struck down by a fatal heart attack at
London Airport – how often death awaits the peripatetic, jet-
setting Greeks at the end of a journey! – George R. Vergottis,
the tanker's owner, accompanied by his mourning brother
Panaghis, was going home for the last time.

Slowly, the funeral procession made its way across the
attractive island, passing the rich and fertile valleys with olive
groves and orange orchards, the scent of fir trees wafting from
the mountainside and filling the air with a resinous tang.
The journey ended at Kourkoumelata, the village of the
Vergottis family. After a religious service, the body of George
Vergottis was committed to the family vault to rest in the
hallowed soil of Cephalonia.

Seven cities claim to have given birth to Homer – if he ever
lived. Cephalonia's boast is probably as valid as Ithaca's. But
whether the larger of the two islands has inspired Homer's
epics or not, there is no doubt about Lord Byron's enchant-

ment with Cephalonia and with Metaxata, the charming village south of Argostolion. From his window Byron looked out on 'the calm though cool serenity of a beautiful and transparent Moonlight showing the Islands, the Mountains, the Sea, the double Azure of the waves and skies,' but almost in the same breath flayed the Greeks whose internecine quarrels marred the spirit of the 1821 revolution: 'The worst of them is', he wrote, 'that they are such damned liars; there never was such an incapacity for veracity since Eve lived in Paradise.'

Greek islanders must have reformed since Byron's days for – to linger in Metaxata before returning to Kourkoumelata – I owe the most accurate and graphic account of Cephalonia's shipping history to a man whose ancestors played host to Byron in Metaxata. Captain Nicolas Basil Metaxas is a small, wiry octogenarian sea captain without whose reminiscences, sparked by an astonishing memory, the story of modern Cephalonia could not have been pieced together. It has been lovingly recorded by his son Basil N. Metaxas, a maritime economist and consultant to the United Nations and the World Bank.

Talking in his pleasant third-floor apartment in the centre of Athens where he lives in retirement, the old sea-dog sailed through over a century of Metaxas and Vergottis shipping history with total recall. Eye witness and participant for more than seven decades, he went back to the very origin of the name he shares with his native village.

'*Metaxa* is the Greek word for silk', he chuckled, 'and the story goes that the first to be known by my name were Greeks from Constantinople who went to China and stole silk worms. They hid them in hollow sticks, brought them back to Constantinople and took them along when they fled to Cephalonia and settled in the place which is now the village of Metaxata. They made their homes in the mountains because pirates were raiding the shores of Cephalonia so frequently that people did not dare to live by the sea.

Although Cephalonia was not quite as barren as other Greek islands, many young men turned to the sea for a livelihood. Cephalonia shipping grew like that of Ithaca next door. What

Theophilatos was for Ithaca, Vaglianos, a prosperous grain merchant, was for Cephalonia. Every member of the Vaglianos family had a ship named after him or her. Soon after the Suez Canal was inaugurated, they opened an office in London which looked after their grain business and expanded into banking and insurance. Anxious to be more than sea captains, their ambition was to become 'captains of industry'. Other Cephalonians – Avgerinos, Botsaris, Lykiardopoulo, Yanoulatos, Rossolimos – were operating their own *lotkas* (sailing ships) as well and only waiting to go over to steam.

In 1955, at the age of eleven Basil Metaxas, Captain Nic's father, left the local Academy (school) to go to sea: 'Father was not paid, not at the beginning. Working hard and sleeping on deck for two years, he qualified for his first wage, fifty francs a month, the equivalent of about £2 in English money. He was determined to educate himself – Cephalonia was a cultured island, more advanced than other islands whose inhabitants did not bother much about education. Father wanted to learn and, however arduous and tiring the work, spent every free minute reading manuals. He studied and studied.

'He observed his masters and learnt from them. Captains still marked positions on maps with wax and sailed by experience. This is how father was taught seamanship. He was twenty when he took the Ministry of Marine examination and received his Master's Certificate. His first ship, the 700 ton wooden schooner, *Ekatarina Sevastopoulo* (the name of the owners), carried wheat and grain from Russia to Britain and was always listing. The crew of fourteen or fifteen men and boys were Cephalonians and stayed on board for years on end. The captain's privilege was to carry a small cargo on his own account from port to port, sell and buy as best he could, a useful extra source of income.

'The round trip from the Sea of Azov to the east coast of Britain and back to Constantinople took four months. Cephalonia was not on the route and father did not get home for years. It was vital to keep the ship out of the Sea of Azov which was frozen up in winter and not to be caught by the ice. If he succeeded, the crew was allowed to make their own way home to Cephalonia.'

Captain Metaxas saved most of his pay until he was able to buy a house in Metaxata. For a bachelor he was getting on in years and was nearly forty before he took time off to propose to a pretty girl from the neighbouring village of Keramiae. Penelope was seventeen when they were married. Best man was Rokos Vergottis, master of another Sevastopoulo ship, who came from Kourkoumelata, the third in the cluster of villages.

A handsome man, tall, strong, with a bushy moustache, Rokos was fond of the ladies even after he was married to another local girl by the name of Felicity who was fiercely jealous and frequently had reason to be. Local husbands did not trust Rokos either, also with good reason. One of them challenged him to a duel but Rokos drew himself up to his full height and hissed: 'I'll blow you off your feet!' There was no duel.

The lives of Captains Vergottis and Metaxas ran along similar lines. Both raised large families – between 1886 and 1908 nine little Metaxas came into the world and over the same period Felicity bore Rokos Vergottis eight children.

In 1892, at the age of eight, little Nic, eldest of the Metaxas brood, was shipped off to Constantinople and enrolled at Robert College, an American school on a hill overlooking the Bosporus, which taught English, French and Latin. The boys were fascinated by ships, knew the outline of every vessel that passed and waved their handkerchiefs in salute. The ships blew their whistles in acknowledgment.

Nic liked the school but looked forward to holidays at home and a few weeks of lazing and lounging, rowing and swimming. It was not to be: 'Father belonged to the old school and did not think young boys ought to have an easy time', he recalled. Nic was put to work on ships, taught to steer, read maps and other tricks of the trade. He was nearly seventeen when he graduated from school but there was no respite, on the contrary. The day he left college he went straight aboard father's

ship *Aenos*, a 2,800 tonner, which left Constantinople the following day for Novosibirsk.

On his first day at sea the boy ventured on to the bridge:
'What are you doing out here?' father barked. 'Take off
your shoes! Bring the *papazi!*' 'I don't understand . . .'
Papazi, Greek for clotter, Nic was told, was a bundle of ship
ropes used to wipe the deck. He came to know the *papazi* well.

'I was learning the hard way,' he said: His nautical education continued in the *Constantinos* and the *Keramiae* in which he
sailed to North African and Black Sea ports. 'Conditions were
not too bad. Whenever we were in port we had fresh meat and
bread; at sea we had biscuits and canned salt beef. I did not
mind the salt beef but, when eaten as a regular diet over a long
period it could cause rheumatism and eye and kidney troubles.'

The year young Metaxas left Robert College, Panaghis Vergottis, the second of Rokos' sons, was enrolled. Within a couple
of years Panaghis and Nic joined the *Annika*, which was owned
by Rokos Vergottis and captained by Panaghis' brother
Gerassimo. Presently the long arm of the older Metaxas
reached out for young Nic. Though he received no pay Captain
Basil Metaxas thought his boy was being treated too well,
too softly: 'Move to another ship and learn discipline!' he
ordered. Obediently, Nic joined the Italian *Caracciolo*, a huge
three-master whose model has a place of honour by the side
of his desk: 'She taught me a lot!'

The most educational trip was a difficult passage to North
America! 'One got to know the currents of the Atlantic and
learned how to get the Trade Winds and Gulf Stream.'
Captain Nic recalled as if it had happened the other day.
'One became part of nature . . . I watched and learned. The
narrow passages were the most difficult to negotiate. The wind
was so low, it took seventeen days from the south-east coast
of Spain to Gibraltar. Sailing close to the shore by night to
get the wind we gained a few miles. By day the western current
carried us back again. Suddenly, an easterly wind blew up
and hustled us past Gibraltar at a speed of thirteen knots, so
fast we overtook the *Caronia*, the big Cunarder!'

What more could Nic do to perfect his seamanship? With a healthy respect for the British naval tradition, he was certain the English could teach him a thing or two. The answer was an English cargo boat plying between North America and Britain: 'I did not mention my previous service and signed on as an ordinary able seaman. It was a great experience. On Greek ships there were no fixed hours, no food regulations, no discipline. The British taught me discipline. The food was not good but the regulations were. The owners felt an obligation to the crew which was something new to me. The pay was better. The Greeks, the French, all Europeans paid sailors sixty francs, £2.40 a month. The British paid me £3.50'

When they made port in Britain, the English crew dispersed and went home. To pick up news from home, Nic went to Cardiff which was swarming with Greeks who made the most of their shore leave, played cards, gambled and took up with girls: 'I didn't,' Captain Nic said, 'I was afraid of catching a disease.' He moved into a Greek boarding house and was looking around for another English ship when he ran into Lambros Vergottis, master of the 4,800 Greek-flag *Proodos* (Progress): 'Why do you want an English ship?' Lambros asked. 'You come with me!' Nic joined *Proodos* as second mate.

Returning to port, he learned that the Vergottis family had sold the *Annika*. With the proceeds plus a little extra, altogether about £12,000, they had bought a bigger, second-hand vessel which they named *Rokos* after Vergottis senior. Master of the *Rokos* was Gerassimo, and first officer was Panaghis Vergottis. Once more Nic Metaxas was recruited for a Vergottis ship and sailed with the *Rokos* until she reached Constantinople.

Metaxas and Vergottis were in and out of each other's ships, fathers, sons, brothers, cousins switching jobs in a game of nautical musical chairs which went on for years. But somehow, while the Vergottis fleet grew and the family launched companies as prolifically as ships and became multi-millionaires, the Metaxas family, though by no means paupers, never reached the Vergottis summit of great wealth. Perhaps, Captain

Nic said wistfully, they lacked what shipowners need apart from a love of ships – financial genius and a passion for money.

There was already a great deal of money about in the villages of Metaxata, Keramiae and Kourkoumelata. The shipping transactions of the local captains involved substantial amounts. In the summer of 1907, Captain Basil Metaxas went to England to take over the 4,600 ton *Daybreak* in Sunderland. Travelling overland from the Sea of Azov, Nic joined his father in London where they put up at an hotel off Piccadilly.

Nic inspected the vessel in Sunderland and reported that all was correct, whereupon Captain Basil went to the bank carrying his money in a big bag. He put it on the counter – £14,000 in gold sovereigns. *Daybreak*, renamed *Livadho* (after the district of the family's native villages) was taken over by Captain Basil, Nic going along as first mate. They loaded coal, sailed to Marseilles and on to Russia to take on a cargo of grain.

Their shipping operations were so successful that it did not take Captains Vergottis and Metaxas long to become so well off that they could afford to retire from the sea. While retaining his financial interests in ships, Captain Metaxas settled down in Cephalonia. Captain Vergottis, who bought land and took on a small army of local peasants to cultivate it, was held in high esteem and elected Mayor of Livadho for two periods of four years. The young men of the family were as handsome, able, popular and amorous as their father. A brilliant officer, young Panaghis commanded ships without the benefit of a captain's diploma. Gerassimo Vergottis invested £1,500 in a house in Kourkoumelata and proposed to Calliope Cambitsi, one of the prettiest local girls whose father was a landowner and whose brother a wealthy merchant in Keramiae.

Nic Metaxas vividly remembers the fine wedding. Friends and local peasants, over a thousand guests crowded into the house and the grounds for the reception. The girls of the Livadho *haute volée* looked attractive in their elegant gowns: 'Our women dressed in the latest Paris fashion,' Nic Metaxas said. 'They read the French fashion journals – I once went to

the offices of *La Femme* in Paris to pay my sister's subscription
– the number of subscribers from Cephalonia was astonishing.'
Gerassimo's furniture was made by Cephalonia's famous wood
carvers – 'Sculptors, real artists they were!' Precious carpets,
Dresden china and fine silverware filled the house.

Cephalonia's shipowners were doing well. They paid cash
for their ships: 'Loans meant slavery to them,' Captain Nic
said. It was also, alas, true that Greeks still found credit hard
to come by though their ships showed a trading profit of
fifteen to twenty per cent on the invested capital, and paid for
themselves within five or six years. How long was the life of a
ship? 'With the Greeks, it was indefinite,' Captain Nic
admitted. The British worked on the basis of a five per cent
depreciation a year: "We took care of our ships!" the captain
added.

At the end of the new century's first decade, the seesaw of
shipping brought freight rates down. The *Rokos* was laid up
and Nic Metaxas did his national service with the Greek navy
while his brother Gerassimo, as the eldest of the family, was
exempt. After his demobilisation, Nic Metaxas became master
of the *Livadho* and worked her for the next two years when,
having earned a handsome profit, she was sold for the same
amount she was bought for. Her captain was about to travel
to London to look for a 'younger and bigger' steamer when
the first Balkan war broke out and he joined up once more.

Gerassimo Vergottis had his eye on a ship, *Calypso*, which
cost £28,000. For the first time in his career he managed to
get credit – not from a bank but from the owners who accepted
a small amount as down payment. He put Panaghis in charge
and the ship did extremely well; the young master sailed fast,
lost no time turning the vessel round, watched the market
carefully and showed sound judgment in choosing his cargoes.

The outbreak of the Balkan war almost caught *Calypso* in
the Black Sea, and only Panaghis' presence of mind saved her.
He stepped up the ship's speed to the very limit, in the nick of
time before the Turks closed the Bosporus and the Dardenelles.
His feat was worth a fortune. The Balkan war made great

demands on available tonnage and caused a shortage pushing up freight rates and profits which rose to about ten per cent of the capital per voyage. When peace returned to the Balkans rates dropped sharply and owners found it difficult to keep up payments.

Now it was Nic Metaxas' turn to take over as captain of the *Calypso*. His salary was £15 a month, the same as the engineer's, while sailors still had to make do with a wage of £2.40. Andrew Vergottis, a giant of a man and strong as an ox, joined the ship as chief officer and together they sailed the usual routes, Black Sea, Continent of Europe, Bristol Channel.

All Nic Metaxas' friends were buying ships or shares in ships and, across over half a century, he remembers every one of them. Gerassimo Vergottis bought a second one which he named after his mother (*Felicity*), and took over brother-in-law Denis Cambitsi's share in the *Demetrios* which was the fourth ship of his fleet. Metaxas senior picked up a quarter share in the Lykiardopoulo ship *Daphne* and put his eldest son, yet another Gerassimo, in charge.

Nic Metaxas was still master of the *Calypso* when the first world war broke out. His orders were to sail to New Orleans to load grain for Naples but when he arrived in Italy he felt in need of a rest, left the ship and went home to Cephalonia. Gerassimo Vergottis also returned to the island while brother Andrew joined the navy and a third Vergottis, George, stayed in the United States.

After a brief rest in Cephalonia, a new assignment awaited Nic Metaxas. Gerassimo Vergottis asked him to go to the United Kingdom with Panaghis to open a Vergottis office in Cardiff, which was a base for operations in many parts. When news reached the two Greeks that a first-class agency was coming on the market in Marseilles, Nic decided to brave the hostile seas and travel to France to investigate.

On March 22, 1915, he took the Channel ferry from Folkestone wondering what was in store for him. He did not have to wait long. The ship had hardly left port when it was hit by a U-boat's torpedo. Did the U-boat commander have reason to assume that a personage of importance was aboard? Did he have secret information? Was the man the Germans tried to catch or kill an English politician, none other than – as was later whispered – the mighty Lloyd George, soon to become Britain's Minister of Munitions and, eventually, Prime Minister? Was the information correct? They never found out and the British certainly did not enlighten them.

It was a terrible disaster. The ferry was cut in two and one half of the stricken vessel went down. Nic Metaxas was thrown into the sea but managed to keep afloat and reach a rowing boat with a British sailor aboard. They rowed towards the floating remnant of the ship and scrambled aboard. British naval vessels raced to the scene and chased the U-boat away, tugs were called in to tow the rump to port. Over a hundred people lost their lives. As the survivors huddled in the engine room to keep warm, a launch with a high-ranking British naval officer arrived, took the mystery man off the wreck and rushed him away. (To this day Captain Metaxas is convinced that it was Lloyd George but no such incident is mentioned in the Beaverbrook collection of documents and records covering the history of Britain's World War One Prime Minister.)

From the French coast which he reached in a tug boat, Nic Metaxas made his way to Paris. At the small hotel, near the Place de l'Opera which he and his friends frequented, he found Panaghis Vergottis in tears. His old friend had gone to France as soon as he had the news of the Channel tragedy to make enquiries about his fate. What he was told led him to fear the worst. He was convinced that Nic Metaxas had perished in the disaster. They had a joyful reunion.

The news from home was grim. Nic felt he ought to go back and see if he could help. Cephalonia was starving. Desperately trying to find food for the hapless island, Admiral Ernest Malcour, the French naval commander in charge, called Cephalonia's prominent citizens together to discuss what could be done to relieve the situation. The most urgent need was for money – it was quickly forthcoming. The island's leading shipowners, Nicholas Lykiardopoulo, Gerassimo Vergottis and

Constantine Mazarakis, put up funds to finance an expedition to Egypt.

The man chosen to lead the rescue operation was Captain Nic Metaxas. If he could get through to Alexandria there might yet be hope. One of the ships laid up in the harbour was put at his disposal. He was given £9,000 in cash to take with him – and a free hand to buy whatever he could find: 'If you can get two bags of onions, you will save human lives,' Nicholas Lykiardopoulo told him. After a hazardous voyage which required courage and skill, Captain Nic Metaxas reached Egypt safely. In Alexandria he was given a sympathetic hearing and found people anxious to co-operate. He spent three months buying up quantities of rice, maize and lentils – no onions – before returning to Cephalonia. The island was saved from starvation.

In Cardiff, in the meantime, Panaghis Vergottis made intelligent use of the family's ships which were mostly employed carrying food from South America to Britain. Risky but extremely profitable, each voyage across the Atlantic taking between three and four months, earned between £15,000 and £20,000. Ships were minting money. *Calypso* and *Rokos* were sold and the proceeds invested in two smaller ships, the 1,500 ton *Aris* and the 3,600 ton *Panaghis*. Vergottis also acquired the Greek-flag *Calimeris* which was originally intended for a Norwegian owner who could not keep her because it was not possible to change from one flag to another in war-time. Nic Metaxas transacted the deal which produced a profit of £30,000.

Their appetite for ships was growing and Gerassimo Vergottis and Nic Metaxas were constantly on the look-out for new vessels but prices were high. Shipowners are cagey about the details of their deals and profits but the amounts involved speak for themselves. When the British offered 'Standard' ships at £250,000, this kind of money was no longer beyond Gerassimo's reach. He bought one and named her *Calypso II*, and made a down-payment on a second which was still under construction and went for £320,000 – she became the *Rokos*

Vergottis. Both vessels kept busy and paid handsome dividends adding to the profits which Gerassimo amassed as he steered adroitly through the financial rapids of the post-war period.

A very rich man, he made the *Ritz* Hotel his permanent London residence and lived the life of a *grand seigneur*. A barber attended him every morning. One day, however, early in 1922, the sharp razor slipped inflicting a slight cut on Gerassimo's face. The wound refused to heal and became septic. Severe blood poisoning developed and spread quickly, Gerassimo never recovered. After his death the flourishing shipping business he had built up was taken over by his brothers, Panaghis, George and Andrew.

For once, it was his own family which laid claim to Captain Nic Metaxas' services. In partnership with his brother Gerassimo and other relatives, he bought a ship called *Margarita*, took over her management and let brother Gerassimo sail as her captain. Confined to shore after half a lifetime at sea, Captain Nic married at long last. His bride was a Cephalonian lady Katerine Razi, they soon had a son who grew up into a fine young man and became an outstanding marine economist and historian. The future looked bright but the cruel sea had a severe shock in store for the family.

With Captain Gerassimo Metaxas at the helm and a crew of thirty-seven Cephalonians aboard, the *Margarita* was crossing the Indian Ocean when she ran into a storm and capsized. Captain and crew went down with the ship. Under the impact of the tragedy, Nic decided to leave the sea for good and joined Vergottis as Marine Superintendent supervising the company's ships, organising repairs and provisions and looking after captains and crews.

As the centre of shipping shifted to London, the Vergottis office moved to the capital but in the late twenties the zip went out of shipping and Panaghis Vergottis began to diversify and invest in other enterprises leaving brothers George and Andrew to carry on the family business. Gerassimo's son Rokos established his own firm, Adelphi Vergottis, which took over control of *Rokos*, *Calypso II*, *Eftikia* and *Aris* – the *Aris* was later sold and replaced with a new ship named after his father.

With the income from his shares in ships big enough to allow him to follow his own inclinations, Gerassimo's younger son Panaghis junior followed intellectual pursuits, taught himself to paint, developed an interest in music, wrote a book on astronomy and mastered other esoteric subjects, inevitably attracting the bewildered comments which Greek shipowners reserve for youngsters who are not exclusively interested in running ships and making money.

George and Andrew Vergottis continued on their own – George bought four ships, *Argeon*, *Ionian*, *Ikarion* and another *Rokos*, Andrew Vergottis ran two, the 5,500 ton *Mimas*, named after his German-born wife, and the 9,000 ton *Cephalonia*.

In the Greek exodus from London in 1939, George Vergottis went to New York taking Nic Metaxas with him to manage the business and buy new ships (the 4,000 ton *Eureka* and her sister ship *Wellington*). Like most Greek vessels in the United States, they sailed under a flag of convenience – the flag of Panama. *Mimas* was sunk by the Germans; *Rokos*, *Argeon*, *Ionian* and *Ikarion* were torpedoed. *Wellington* en route from the Amazon to New York, came to grief in the Caribbean.

Compensation for war-time losses which put most Greek owners on their feet again, did not come to Vergottis without a fight. The insurance companies offered Greek currency which was not much use in the post-war era and Vergottis went to court to demand payment in pound sterling. They won their case. Three Liberty ships replaced some of their losses and soon traded under new classical names: *Dimosthenis*, *Themistocles* and *Perikles*.

For Captain Nic Metaxas it was the end of the road. He left the States and returned to Athens to live in busy semi-retirement while the family shipping interests were administered by a London-based firm. From the sea to the good earth – he took up farming in Cephalonia, installed cisterns to gather rain for irrigation, and has been tilling his land as fondly as he steered his ships.

The Vergottis fleet steamed on and grew apace with Greek

shipping. Not one to miss out on a boom, Panaghis rediscovered his love for shipping – few islanders can keep their hands off ships for long – and launched a new firm, Valiant Steamship Company, which concentrates on the smaller-size Virgo ships. Like brother Gerassimo before him, he settled in a permanent suite at the London *Ritz* and occupied a regular lunch table at the 'Greek shipowners' canteen' (*Claridge's* hotel), the richest fountain of shipping gossip in the world. Every summer, he went back to the old house in Kourkoumelata where his brother joined him.

It came as a fearful blow to the old gentleman when an earthquake ravaged Cephalonia in 1953 and completely destroyed their native village. George Vergottis promptly put up six million drachmae – £100,000 – to bring Kourkoumelata back to life, more modern and with vastly improved utilities. Other Cephalonians, particularly Lykiardopoulo and Marchessinis, were not far behind with generous contributions. The Vergottis house rose from the ruins in new splendour and old Captain Nic lovingly rebuilt his home.

Age and illness were beginning to take their toll of the old ones. The health of the once-powerful Andrew Vergottis was failing. Doctors could not help and he went to live in the South of France where he died in 1964. Panaghis, though older, was fit and well but taking life easier. One of his dearest friends was Aristotle Onassis whose Ionian hang-up brought him closer to the ageing Cephalonian than to any other Greek shipowner. Had it not been for Onassis, Panaghis might have continued to live in obscurity as the code of the traditional Greeks demands. It was not to be, and soon their two names were linked in a blaze of publicity.

There was as yet not a cloud over their thirty-years old friendship when Panaghis Vergottis attended the spectacular dinner at the *Dorchester Hotel* in London which Onassis gave in honour of Maria Callas to celebrate her appearance as Media at Covent Garden in July 1959. Not a hint of Vergottis' affection for Callas nor of Onassis' infatuation with the American-born Greek diva.

The following summer *Christina* sailed in Cephalonian waters, and among Onassis' friends aboard was Maria Callas – and Panaghis Vergottis: 'He is one of my dearest friends,' Onassis told Callas, 'if not the best I have.' The trio met frequently in London, in Paris, in Athens. Panaghis joined the ranks of Callas admirers and camp followers and the years, if anything, intensified their feelings for each other: 'As a Greek he participated in my glory,' Maria said later, 'I was his greatest joy.' She came to love Vergottis: 'He was more than a father,' she said. 'I am forty-three, he is now seventy-seven . . . Mr Onassis is younger, so that is another relationship,' she added.

The talk between them was of ships, naturally, and the rich fund of shipping anecdotes and the glamour of multi-million dollar transactions fascinated the great diva. She was, she said, reaching a point in her life when she was anxious to invest her money profitably: 'I am a woman who works for a living,' was how she explained her position, 'and, coming towards an age when it may not be possible to work, I wanted to make sure of a comfortable income!' With friends like Onassis and Vergottis her thoughts inevitably turned to shipping as an answer to her prayer and she decided to buy a ship, or at least, a share in a ship – with Onassis and Vergottis as partners in the venture.

To make a long, complicated and rather unpleasant story short, 'her dear friend Vergottis' found a suitable ship for her. The 27,000 ton *Artemision II*, which was being built at El Ferrol in Spain, was available for around £1.4 million and could probably be acquired for a little less. Callas was so excited she wanted to go to El Ferrol at once to see the ship but was persuaded to entrust the transaction to Vergottis. She immersed herself in the highly technical subjects of credit facilities, charters, freight rates and all the other paraphernalia of the trade. A Liberian corporation, Overseas Bulk Carriers, was

Five Kulukundis brothers and their partners. Back row (*l to r*): John E. G. Kulukundis, Nicholas E. Kulukundis, George E. Kulukundis, Michael E. Kulukundis; front row: Manuel E. Kulukundis, Minas B. Rethymnis, B. M. Mavroleon

formed to buy the *Artemision* at a final price of £1.2 million –
down payment: ten per cent.

The three partners agreed on a scheme under which Callas
was to produce £60,000 of the down payment and get a twenty-
five per cent share of the ship, Vergottis another twenty-five and
Onassis fifty per cent of which he proposed to transfer twenty-
six per cent to Callas to give her a fifty-one per cent majority.
Callas, Onassis and Vergottis dined together at *Maxim's* in
Paris to celebrate the deal. They had little to celebrate. Teeth-
ing troubles delayed the *Artimision's* first tour of duty between
the West Coast of America and Japan. There were more setbacks with faulty signals and with a deck-motor which broke
down and had to be replaced: 'She is an unlucky ship,'
Vergottis told Maria Callas.

They discussed changes in the arrangements but Callas
did not like the suggestion that, this being such a risky venture,
her down-payment should be regarded as a loan, to be repaid
with interest. She would not hear of it and wanted control of
the ship. Another business matter on which Vergottis advised
her was a contract for a German version of Tosca but Onassis
intervened and arguments developed. The happy father-
daughter relationship between 'Pan' and Maria came under
a strain. One of their many telephone conversations de-
generated into an ascerbic quarrel but when Callas tried to
make it up, Vergottis would not be mollified. His heart died
there and then, he said.

The last love of an old man turned into bitterness. Onassis
wanted the *Artemision* partnership put on a strict business basis
but Vergottis was too angry to agree to anything. He turned
down a proposal to submit the matter to legal arbitration.
Dealings between Onassis and Vergottis became more and
more acrimonious. Onassis was convinced that his old crony
wanted to drag him and Maria Callas into court. The simmer-
ing hostility erupted in the dining room of *Claridge's* when
Onassis walked over to Vergotti's table to be received with an
angry shout: 'Get out of here!' – Vergottis raised a bottle of
whisky – 'or I'll throw it at you.' Onassis was stunned: 'You

are crazy!' he muttered and walked away. They had spent half a lifetime talking to each other. They never talked again.

The dispute came up in the London Law Courts in the Spring of 1967. It was a nasty case. The argument was largely about Callas' down payment – did it entitle her to a share of the ship, as she and Onassis claimed, or was it, as Vergottis contended, a loan? It was London's *cause célèbre* of the year. A small army of reporters and as many lawyers as could cram into the court room watched Callas in the witness box. Their curiosity was richly rewarded. Her appearance owed little to her most captivating performance on stage. She looked handsome, elegant, proud and her impromptu lines were more pungent than some of her stage dialogue. Onassis was as fiery as ever but Panaghis Vergottis looked very old and fragile.

The testimony of the principals, as all shipping talk, was peppered with references to love and marriage. But, in the idiom of shipowners, the terms were applied to the ship. Onassis remarked that Vergottis had not been the only one flirting with her – the *Artemision*. Counsel retorted that the ship was off the market: 'So long as the girl is not married she is still free,' was Onassis' rejoinder. There was laughter in court when Counsel answered: 'If the ship is on the market, until the lady is married, the celebration dinner at *Maxim's* was before the wedding – because the marriage deal had not gone through.' Onassis: 'Excuse me, the marriage was announced, and all that was needed was a doctor's certificate.' One of the personal aspects into which the argument strayed was an alleged quarrel between Callas and Onassis. Vergottis' lawyers brought up the incident but tactful handling of the case prevented other invasions into the private lives of the contestants.

The Judge's verdict at the end of the proceedings was in favour of Onassis and Callas. Onassis described it as 'the humiliation of an old friend which I bitterly regret'. Vergottis contested the decision and appealed to a higher court which brought the costs of the proceedings up to £50,000. The lower court's judgment was upheld.

Not long after losing his oldest friend Panaghis Vergottis lost his brother George who died in London. George Vergottis left a fleet of twelve brand new dry cargo vessels and tankers, ranging from 15,000 to 40,000 tons, half of them to his widow, who moved from the *Ritz* in London to the *Grande Bretagne* in Athens, and commutes between Greece and the United States. Some of the ships went to Panaghis who continued in shipping and visited his offices most afternoons.

His last years were sad and lonely. The bitterness lingered, and pride prevented him from making up the quarrel with his old friend even after Onassis parted from Callas and married Jackie Kennedy. The two men came frequently face to face lunching at *Claridge's* – at separate tables – but neither took the short step across the gulf of jealousy which had become meaningless. One of Panaghis Vergottis' last acts was another generous donation to his beloved Cephalonia – £150,000 to build a school, The Vergottis Public School for Merchant Marine Captains. A few days after returning from Pireaus where he handed over the cheque in a public ceremony, he fell ill in his apartment at the London *Ritz*. He never recovered.

The younger generation of the family took over where their elders had left off, less personal (and, perhaps, less dedicated to Cephalonia) but more methodical in their approach, computers replacing intuition and legal agreements the handshakes with which the old captains sealed their bargains. Running ships became a matter of steering committees rather than steering wheels. The young captains are more at home in the boardroom than on the bridge. They are no less capable for all that.

XIV

1965-1972: 440 MILLION DOLLARS

MINOS Colocotronis was nervously fumbling with his watch. The special aircraft taking him and seventy or eighty of his guests from London to Newcastle was late taking off. A mix-up at the last count delayed departure because there were two more people aboard than figured on the passenger list. In these days of highjackers . . . another count, a re-count, checking with ground staff, radio calls to the other two special aircraft already on their way resolved the mystery but the vital half hour's delay could not be made up.

An hour later, on arrival at Newcastle, Minos Colocotronis conducted his fellow passengers to the coaches waiting to take them on to Sunderland and the launching of the latest addition to his fleet of tankers and bulk cargo ships. The coach drivers stepped hard on the accelerators but however skilfully they navigated the heavy traffic on the congested roads of the industrial north of England, they were bound to be late.

When the convoy arrived at Sunderland Docks, the launching, meticulously timed to catch the tide in the mouth of the River Wear within the ten minutes it was high enough to float the ship, was over and done with. Minos Colocotronis could just see his new vessel disappearing in the distance. It was probably the only time in the seven fantastic years when his fleet grew from nothing to two and a quarter million tons (and a value of 450 million dollars), that he had missed anything, anything at all.

The launching of a ship is like the birth of a baby that comes into the world fully grown and capable of earning the parents a handsome income. There may have been problems in the period of gestation with timing, finance, design, raw materials, labour relations and charters – no, not charters, they are arranged even before the ship is commissioned – and the birth may have been a difficult one but once the vessel is ready to take to sea all is forgotten.

This is the moment when shipowners make as much fuss as possible to give the newcomer a rousing welcome – no trouble or money spared. In this spirit, the directors of Colocotronis Limited (in association with the builders Austin & Pickersgill) sent out invitations to some two hundred and fifty friends, business associates and their wives, sons and daughters to attend the launching of *Santa Vassiliki* from the Southdock Shipyard at Sunderland on April 7, 1971, and a formal dinner-dance at the *Gosforth Park Hotel*, Newcastle that same evening.

To convey the guests from London, Colocotronis hired a special train – rooms for two hundred and fifty were booked in the best Newcastle hotel. Because of a threatening strike arrangements were changed in the nick of time and there aircraft were hired to take the party from London to the north.

Jollifications started at Gatwick Airport where caviare and Champagne were served to put the guests in the right frame of mind. German, French and British shipping men, bankers, insurance brokers, industrialists, and technicians mingled with the large Greek contingent. The nucleus of the gathering was a family affair revolving around Madame Vassiliki Colocotonis, mother of Minos and Joseph, the firm's principals, who would perform the launching ceremony and give her name to the ships.

Costa and John Hadjipateras were there – their sister is Mrs Minos Colocotronis. As executives of Colocotronis Limited, Antony and Alec Georgiadis, the owners' nephews, played their part. The proprietor of the shipyard, jovial, jolly Basil Mavroleon was much in evidence – his son-in-law Charles Longbottom, managing director of Austin & Pickershill, was waiting at the other end with the shipyard workers employed in the Colocotronis vessel.

The first two aircraft took off on time with their contingents of passengers – it was just as well that Joseph Colocotronis and the ship's godmother were aboard. They joined the guests on the big stand built for the occasion. Madame Colocotronis broke the obligatory bottle of champagne on the bow of the ships and named her *Santa Vassiliki*.

The handsome vessel, a 15,000 ton dry cargo ship of the highly successful SD 14 type in which the yard specialises, cost some £1.5 million and took eight months to complete. She was already on charter to a German company. One of a series of nine Colocotronis ships on order, the *Santa Vassiliki* was the first instalment of a £15 million operation for owners and builders.

Charles Longbotton made a speech, and, in the (temporary) absence of Minos Colocotronis, brother Joseph responded. He handed his mother a handsome brooch as a memento and produced a cheque of £1,000 as a donation for the men who built the ship. The visitors moved on to a big marquee for a late buffet lunch before returning to their hotels just in time to change for the dinner-dance which went on until the small hours. The following morning the three aircraft returned them to London.

Small by the standards of the super-tanker era, the *Santa Vassiliki* joined a fleet whose phenomenal growth over the past seven years has been watched with awe by shipping experts all over the world. Starting from scratch in 1964, Colocotronis have created a shipping empire which now ranks fourth in size among the Greeks – after Lemos, Onassis and Niarchos, proving that, for the astute operator, shipping has remained a growth industry second to none.

The quietly elegant Colocotronis offices in Leadenhall Street in the City of London were ticking over smoothly as ever when I visited them at the beginning of my inquiries into this astonishing industrial effort. An undercurrent of excitement, well-controlled but unmistakable, was running through the Operations Room and the Chartering Department with tele-phone calls from Japan, New York, Athens, Hamburg chasing each other. The same mood pervaded the Finance and Accounts departments, and the executive suite presided over by the trim figure of Minos Colocotronis, with the pencil-slim moustache and clever eyes peering through horn-rimmed spectacles. Alec and Tony Georgiadis rushed in and out of the office with tapes from the teleprinter which links headquarters with shipping centres all over the world.

It was a climactic moment, when it is impossible to disguise the inter-action of crisis and profit. The morning's news which galvanised shipping offices and sent freight rates soaring in the world market came from Libya where the ruling Revolution Command Council (which had deposed and supplanted King Idris the previous year) abruptly announced the nationalisation of all oil importing and distribution companies in the country, including Esso-Libya, the Anglo-Dutch Shell Group and a subsidiary of Italy's state-owned Agip. Import, distribution and sale of petroleum products, said Essedin Al-Mabrouk the Minister for Oil and Minerals, would henceforth be handled by the Libyan National Oil Corporation.

For oil companies, such political interventions are regular professional hazards. But, however great a set-back for the oil companies, this sort of move inevitably creates a heavy demand for tanker tonnage which is inseparable from tension and the danger of conflagration. Coming at the time of the Middle East conflict, the Libyan shock measure was typical of events which put a premium on ships.

This is the time when tanker owners scrutinise their charter schedules in the hope of finding some of their ships idle. To have ships without a charter – which they try to avoid in normal times – becomes a licence to print money. That day, at the Colocotronis office, the records revealed a highly satis-factory state of affairs for a shipowner at the time of an inter-national crisis. With the index of charter rates higher (World Scale 200, to use the technical term), than in many a month, some 500,000 tons of Colocotronis shipping was just about to come off charter and was free to be re-chartered at the new top rates.

For Colocotronis – and a few other shipping operators in the same fortunate position – it offered a unique opportunity. To put it as simply as possible – it meant that each of their ships re-chartered at the new record rates could recoup its total cost with two consecutive voyages! In a matter of weeks or, at the most, months, a ship costing a million pounds could earn a million pounds leaving the vessel free of mortgage to earn its price over and over again for years to come. Colocotronis were about to accomplish this financial legerdemain to the tune of 500,000 tons. Had they not already been riding high, this single coincidence of politics and shipping would have been enough to make Minos and Joseph Colocotronis and their associates a fortune overnight.

They were not born poor, not by any means, but such spectacular shipping coups could hardly have been predicted for them at their cradle. What they did inherit at birth was a name which shines bright in modern Greek history. Their ancestor, Theodore Colocotronis, a famous *klephtes* (brigand) in the early nineteenth century when *klephtes* was synonymous with patriot and hero, was a leading freedom fighter in the Greek struggle for independence in 1822 and at one period virtual ruler of the Peloponnese.

His descendant, Minos Colocotronis, was born in Athens in 1919. His father, a banker, had three other children – a boy Joseph and two girls, Clio and Amalia. Minos was fourteen when the family moved to Cairo, where he joined the Jesuit College, was taught French and English, and went on to study mathematics, philosophy and law graduating in all three disciplines, a rare accomplishment.

Even this crowded curriculum was not enough for the ambitious youngster and Minos was constantly on the look-out for new outlets for his energy. He took a job with the Cairo branch of the French bank, Credit Lyonais, yet still found time to row and swim in the Nile, play tennis with the sons and daughters of the international set – English, French, Greek, Italians – which gave the Egyptian capital its cosmopolitan flavour.

When the versatile and well-connected young man joined the Free Greek Forces in the second world war, he was assured of quick promotion. His first assignment was to the office of Prime Minister George Papandreou who was smuggled out of Greece to head his country's exile government in Cairo. Joseph Colocotronis joined the Greek commandos as a parachutist and distinguished himself in battle. Clio Colocotronis married Vassos Georgiadis, a Greek from Smyrna who settled in Kampala, Uganda, where he made a fortune in tobacco and where their sons Alec and Antony were born.

There was as yet not a whiff of the sea, not a hint of shipping, in the lives of Minos and Joseph Colocotronis. After the war Minos went to Paris to continue his studies. He was spending his first post-war holiday with friends in Switzerland, staying at the *Richemond Hotel* in Geneva, when he was introduced to the handsome Katingo Hadjipateras, daughter of Adamantios and sister of Costa and John. They fell in love and were married in Lausanne the following year. Their son John was born in Paris in 1951.

Ancient Greek shipping clans like the Pateras-Hadjipateras do not take kindly to outsiders. Minos Colocotronis was one of the exceptions. Katingo's husband had obvious talents which could be most usefully employed. He was invited to join Hadjipateras shipping firm – provided he was content to start as an apprentice. Minos Colocotronis accepted with alacrity. He moved to London, where he and his wife settled down to a pleasant existence. Supplementing his salary with his own income and the proceeds of his wife's share in the business, he applied himself to his job. For the learned apprentice there was much to learn.

A compact, active firm, steeped in tradition but alert to modern techniques, important in shipping but not so big as to deny a clever employee an overall view of the business, the Hadjipateras office was ideal training ground. There was no branch of the trade in which the newcomer could not gain experience. Accounts, Insurance, Chartering, Purchasing – Minos worked his way through every department. And the rewards of shipping could be high even for an employee. Before long, Minos and Katingo could well afford to move into one of London's choicier quarters. The new apartment overlooking Hyde Park reflected the progress in the career of the ambitious operator.

Seeing a Greek shipping man at work, one does not require a vivid imagination to guess his thoughts and his aims in life. What Minos Colocotronis was dreaming of while helping to manage Hadjipateras ships, was a ship of his own or rather two, three, four, five Colocotronis ships – a whole Colocotronis fleet. To start a shipping dynasty to hand down to his son who was at school in London – as were cousins, Alec and Tony Georgiadis whose father died in the early fifties.

Clio Colocotronis-Georgiadis had been a widow for eight years when she told her sons that she intended to marry again: 'We were grown up', Tony Georgiadis recalled, 'and very happy with her decision. We thought mother should lead a full life.' Clio's second husband was Sir Frederick Crawford, Governor and Commander in Chief of Uganda from 1957 until independence (when he settled in Rhodesia). The boys were at St Edmund Hall, Oxford, Alec reading Law, Tony taking Philosophy and Economics. Both graduated with honours and went on to Columbia University to take degrees in business administration.

They were still in the United States when their uncle Minos Colocotronis, after fifteen years as a learner and wage earner, worked up a powerful head of steam which propelled him towards independence: 'By 1965', said Minos, 'I felt I knew enough about shipping to start up on my own.' In partnership with brother Joseph he started a shipping firm taking his sisters, Lady Clio Crawford and Amalia into the venture with him.

The pattern was almost an exact replica of the beginnings of the London Greeks. Though conditions and techniques had changed considerably. Colocotronis in the sixties operated very much like Kulukundis forty years earlier. One vital difference was that Greek shipping had acquired prestige which it sorely lacked in the twenties. Equally as important was that opportunities were greater, dimensions infinitely bigger, and amounts involved a multiple of the capital Greeks invested in the inter-war years.

'We began in a one-room office in Leadenhall Street, one room and two employees,' Minos Colocotronis said – one could almost hear Manuel Kulukundis speaking of 1921. Approaching his project with intimate knowledge of the market and the reputation of a sound and solid shipping executive, he yet set himself only a modest objective: 'We were not over-ambitious," he added. 'We looked for suitable ships, small ones!' For the down payments they drew on the family funds in Swiss banks.

The new firm's first ship was a 17,500 ton tanker, named *Katingo*, the inevitable compliment a Greek shipowner pays his wife. There were no problems with banks and insurance institutions, and the response from oil companies was equally reassuring. The consensus of opinion was the experienced Greek operators would run their ships efficiently and deliver the goods – in every sense of the word. *Katingo* was chartered by the Belgian oil company Petro-Fina and carried her first cargo of crude petroleum from the Caribbean to Europe. The second Colocotronis ship, a 5,000 ton dry cargo vessel, *Lady Clio*, found employment as quickly.

Discounting the charter, Colocotronis proceeded to their next ship, sixteen years old 15,000 ton *Mitsera Vassiliki*, and yet another one, more than double the size, twelve years old and named *Sir Frederick* – after Clio's husband. As the fleet grew, so did the home base. Although the market declined and conditions were unstable, largely due to the war in Vietnam, the arm moved to a six-room office further up Leadenhall Street. Before long the Colocotronis office occupied the whole floor, and a second floor, and the staff numbered sixty-five. Lady Clio's sons, the Georgardis brothers, armed with their American degrees, became full partners.

With the market perking up again, the Colocotronis build-up continued. Following in the footsteps of Petro-Fina and

Esso, other leading oil companies – British Petroleum, Shell, Gulf Oil (Paul Getty's firm), Gelsenburg, Mobile, Texaco and Total – chartered Colocotronis ships: 'They knew they could rely on good service, performance and punctuality,' Minos Colocotronis remarked with natural pride. European and American finance institutes gave him their support.

In 1967, Joseph Colocotronis took charge of the firm's new office in Piraeus and threw himself into work and play with typical Greek gusto. An enthusiastic party-goer, he frequently did not get home to his rather impressive house in Kifizia before the early hours but still reached the office religiously at five a.m. for a full day's work.

The growth of the fleet was steady and consistent Eight new ships were added in 1967, nine more the following year. The 1969 tally was another thirteen, each incorporating Colocotronis in her name. The series started with *Leader Colocatronis* and *Epic Colocotronis* and continued with even grander combinations like *Dynamic Colocotronis, Majestic Colocotronis, Historic Colocotronis*. The 85,700 ton *General Colocotronis*, marked the ascent into the super-tanker category. *Chief Colocotronis* went even further – to 91,100 tons.

Every shipping success can be traced back to a technique which is the operator's speciality. In retrospect, it often looks quite simple, as with Onassis opting for ever bigger vessels and starting the rush of tankers towards the million ton mark; but every radical new departure invites risks and requires courage.

Behind the Colocotronis advance was also a seemingly simple philosophy which overcame one of the principal hazards of the shipping game, the time factor. A shortage of tonnage and a buoyant market sends owners scurrying around the shipyards ordering new vessels but conditions often change dramatically while a ship is a-building. It is by no means unusual for a vessel which was ordered in a period of full employment and seemed to have a busy future ahead, to come off the slipway at a time when there is a glut of tonnage and freight rates are tumbling, a phenomenon not unknown in other industries.

In times of shortage everybody produces – and all together produce a glut!

Values fluctuating in the interval between order and delivery can turn a vessel which seemed a good bargain at three million dollars into a white elephant worth no more than half or a third of that amount. Some owners cannot afford to wait until the market perks up again and are forced to pay huge cancellation fees or to take a loss which can be as big as the profits are when times are good.

Minos Colocotronis was determined to avoid this occupational hazard. Rather than enter into huge long-term commitments with shipyards, he put his trust in second-hand vessels. His secret was to buy, take over and employ without the ominous time lag! The search for the best second-hand vessels led him to Norway.

Just when his expansion programme was getting under way, second-hand Norwegian vessels were coming on the market in a better condition than those of almost any other nationality. Norwegians were selling their tankers at an early age because of a peculiarity in their tax regulations which threatened them with crippling demands in respect of earnings from ships which were only a few years old. The tax on a profit of ten million dollars in one year, for instance, amounted to seven or eight million dollars. But if an owner set off a ten million dollar profit against order for new ships costing ten million dollars, there was no tax to pay.

Inevitably, Norwegian owners, having recovered the cost of their ships within three or four years when the profits became subject to tax, sold their ships and bought new ones. At this moment Colocotronis stepped in and bought – second-hand Norwegians. Most of the first batch of Colocotronis ships were of Norwegian origin. As second-hand ships go, they were young – their average age was about eight years.

He would not be a patriotic Colocotronis (*Patriotic Colocotronis* was the name he gave a 61,000 tonner, bought in 1969) if he did not man his ships with Greeks. Chios, Andros, Crete and Cephalonia were the islands from which his crews were drawn. And, when the Greek government made it profitable for owners to operate their ships under the Greek flag, he rallied to the national cause. By 1971, twenty-four Colocotronis ships were registered in Greece and only six sailed under Central American flags of convenience.

Colocotronis operations went so smoothly that their vast and rapid expansion did not attract much public attention – except for a piece in the ever-alert *Time* magazine which listed Minos Colocotronis by the side of Costa M. Lemos among the anonymous 'other Greeks' – other than Onassis and Niarchos While these two names are incessantly bandied about the British public might not have become aware of Colocotronis existence had it not been for the furore caused by a rare visit to London of Sir Frederick and Lady Crawford in May 1968. As a resident of Rhodesia, which became 'enemy territory' after its sensational Unilateral Declaration of Independence (U.D.I.), Sir Frederick said to be closely associated with Rhodesia's 'rebel' Premier Ian Smith, became subject to the British boycott of all things and persons Rhodesian.

Arriving with Lady Clio to attend the wedding of Alec Georgiadis (to young Katingo Pateras whose name tells the story of her background) he was briefly detained by immigration officers and his passport was impounded. His offence, as stated, was 'giving comfort to the illegal regime of Ian Smith'. Rumours linked the Colocotronis shipping firm with Rhodesia and were fed when Ian Smith's stepson Robert came to London as Alec Georgiadis guest.

Lady Crawford who came for dental treatment was refused admission to Britain. The incident developed into a political row in the House of Commons where Sir Alec Douglas Home reproached the Labour Foreign Secretary Michael Stewart for upholding the ban. With the advent of a Tory Government in Britain, the difficulties were resolved. Sir Frederick and Lady Clio slipped quietly into London for a lavish party to celebrate the engagement of Tony Georgiadis to Elita Lanaras, daughter of a wealthy Greek industrialist. A few months later the young couple were married in Athens.

Once more, the names of Colocotronis and Georgiadis disappeared from public view but their shipping colleagues continued to watch their progress with growing interest and respect as Colocotronis profits increased and Minos and his associates became wealthier and wealthier. He told me that wealth has not changed his style of life which is simple – by the standards of millionaire Greek shipowners. He has not changed his London apartment in fifteen years but has added a Swiss chalet at Villars sur Ollon, near Montreux, and a house in the Algarve (Portugal) to his establishments.

With his insatiable appetite for activity, Minos plays tennis at London's *Queens Club* and golf on the course of the Automobile Club but even at tennis or golf he keeps an eye as firmly on business as on the ball. Evenings at home are a continuation of work in another locale. Most of his time is spent on the telephone talking shop and the theme is the same at Greek parties which he attends regularly.

For a Greek shipowner married to a shipowner's daughter, this combination of business and pleasure creates no problems. On the contrary – his son John is already a shipowner in the making. Thoroughly anglicised by his years as a pupil at Westminster School he wears his hair long in the English fashion on which the Greek Colonels frown. Although he swims, rides and skis, most of the young man's holidays are spent on ships. He was at Piraeus when Colocotronis took delivery of their O.B.O. (Ore, Bulk, Oil) carrier *Epic Colocotronis* and, after finishing school in 1969, joined the *General Colocotronis* at Trieste as an ordinary seaman and sailed with her to North Africa and the Persian Gulf.

The next stage of his shipping education was a spell at the offices of the family firm to acquaint himself with the intricacies of chartering and the finer points and techniques of the business. According to his father, he makes do with £1 a week pocket money but father pays all the bills. When last seen, John was heading for Oxford to follow in the footsteps of his cousins.

Like them, he will go to an American university before joining the firm as a partner. Joseph Colocotronis has no son. His three daughters are fast approaching marriageable age and their future husbands can expect formidable dowries.

Colocotronis, of course, no longer confine themselves to second-hand vessels. The Austin & Pickersgill operation, elevated them to the exclusive circle of Greeks whose orders keep the shipyards of England, Germany, France and Japan busy. To limit liability in case of accidents, each ship is controlled by a separate company which has become universal practice since the *Torey Canyon* foundered and sank off the British coast causing grave oil pollution, and her sister ship, belonging to the same company was held liable for the damage.

Like other shipowners, Minos Colocotronis has acquired other interests including considerable real estate, mainly in Greece. But ships are his life: 'We operate them, we charter, we insure – with Lloyds – we collect freights which are deposited in external accounts in English banks and we employ agents in most shipping centres.' Weekends he often visits his ships.

It is an open secret that the major Greek shipowners – Lemos, Onassis, Niarchos – could not have acquired their immense wealth without astute management of their tax affairs. This is equally true of the Colocotronis family. Though they live in England, they are domiciled in Switzerland and Greece: 'On our British earnings', Minos Colocotronis explained, 'we pay tax in Britain.' His flag of convenience ships pay tax in Panama, Honduras or Liberia, as the case may be, which is virtually nil.

Now they can take advantage of the concessions which the Greek Colonels, competing for custom with the 'Panhonlib' countries, have made as an inducement to owners to register their ships in Greece. Though opponents of the Junta say they have transformed Greece into a 'banana republic', there is no doubt that the country, as well as the shipowners, derives considerable benefit from the rapid and spectacular growth of the shipping industry. Who can blame the sentimental, nostalgic, fiercely patriotic heirs of the Greek captains because they have succumbed to the temptations of the new tax concessions and restored their ships to their own country. After all, Odysseus did not pay tax either.

BIBLIOGRAPHY

The Rich and the Super Rich, Ferdinand Lundberg, Thomas, Nelson, London, 1970.

Journey to a Greek Island, Elias Kulukundis, Cassel, London, 1968.

The Merchant Marine of the Hellenes, Stratis Andreadis, Athens, 1964.

The Greek Islands, Ernle Brandford, Collins, London, 1970.

The Story of Modern Greece, C. M. Woodhouse, Faber & Faber, London, 1968.

Autobiography, Konstantine Hadjipateras. Introduced by John A. Hadjipateras, London, 1963.

Venizelos, The Creator of Modern Greece, Doros Alastos, London, 1942.

Those Fabulous Greeks, Doris Lilly, Cowles Book Company, New York, 1970.

Onassis, Willi Frischauer, Bodley Head, London, 1968.

The History of the Chios Navy, G. A. Lemos, Athens 1964.

The Navy of the Greeks, G. A. Lemos, Athens 1965.

Look, *Der Spiegel* (Hamburg), *Sunday Times* (London), *Naftika Chronika* (Athens), etc.

INDEX

INDEX

213

92–93; rumours of quarrels with Ari, 93–94; is accepted as friend by Christina Onassis, 96
Onassis, Tina (*see also* Blandford, Tina), 60, 62, 63, 90
Orlandos, Rodinos, 68, 69
Ormos, 150, 156
Oros Athos, 172

Paloma, 147, 150
Panaghis, 188
Papachristiris, Frixos, 170
Papadopoulos, Premier George, 15, 69, 70, 71
Papandreou, Prime Minister George, 201
Papastratos, Aliki, 150
Paravicini, Camilla, 142
Passalimani, 17
Patakos, Colonel, 15
Pateras, Adamantios, 37, 42
Pateras, Chrysanthi (*see* Lemos, Chrysanthi)
Pateras, Constantine, 43
Pateras, Diamantis, 35, 38, 40, 42, 46
Pateras family (*see also* Hadjipateras family), 14, 21, 31, 32, 39, 42, 43, 46, 49
Pateras, George, 37
Pateras, Irene, 37
Pateras, John, 37
Pateras, John C., 35
Pateras, Katingo (*see* Georgiadis, Katingo)
Pateras, Katingo (wife of Konstantine), 37
Pateras, Katingo (sister of Strovili Lemos), 51–52
Pateras, Konstantine J. early education on Oinoussai, 35; death of father, 35; buys share in first ship, 36; marries Katingo Pateras 37; birth of children, 37; starts own Insurance company, 38; pilgrimage to Jerusalem, 38; adds prefix Hadji to surname, 39; forms association with a Pateras and a Lemos, 39; purchases

Marietta Ralli and *Leandros*, 39; leaves Pateras and Lemos to form partnership with brothers, 40; ships requisitioned for Balkan War and World War I, 41; partnership with brothers dissolved, 42; sons invest in new ships, 42; devotes himself to rebuilding on Oinoussai, 42; death in Athens, 45
Pateras, Maro (*see* Hadjipateras, Maro)
Pateras, Mitsa (*see* Dracoulis, Mitsa)
Pateras, Nicholas, 35, 38, 40, 42, 46, 50
Pateras, Pantelis, 43
Pateras, Peter, 43
Pateras, Rallia, 37
Pateras, Tiki (*see* Hadjipateras, Tiki)
Patriotic Colocotronis, 205
Pauley, Ed, 172
Paul VI, Pope, 49
Pedall, 58
Peloponnese, 14
Pembroke Hill, 134
Pericles, 190
Petingo, 48
Petro-Fina, 203, 204
Petros, 156
Polyktor, 167
Posidonia, 70
Primera, 176
Proodos, 183
Pulman, Jack, 127
Putney Hill, 134

Queen Mary, 140

Radiant I, 138
Radiant II, 140–43
Radziwill, Lee, 93
Razi, Katerine, 189
Rethymnis, Captain Nicholas B., 111, 112, 115, 119, 125, 158
Rethymnis, Minas, 107, 110, 111, 113, 115
Riggs, Alfred H., 175
Rio Grande, 153
R. & K. Lines, 107, 113, 119, 128,

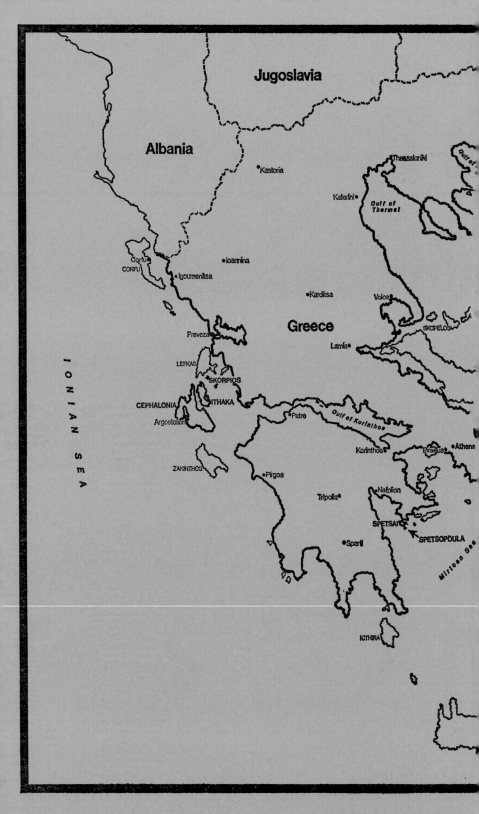